CW01662469

TABLE OF CONTENTS

PART 3
CONVERSIONS

PART 4
THE SOLUTION IS YOU.
BECOMING A WORLD CLASS ENTREPRENEUR

PREFACE

YOU'RE HERE BECAUSE YOU WANT MORE.

More money, more clients, more freedom… and to do so without the confusion, frustration or overwhelm.

"If it were just more information we need, we would all be billionaires with perfect abs".

This quote sums it up perfectly, and why I want to give you the steps and advice along with action taking needed to give you what you want.

Being a trainer, coach or consultant that gets results with your clients, confident with your skills and know-how, but that voice in the back of your head keeps creeping through and telling you that you want more for your life.

I have written this because it can be much simpler than you think when it comes to creating the business that gives you the ability to have the positive impact and give you the money, freedom and lifestyle you want all while doing what you love. This book is written because I want to give you, what I ultimately give all my clients in both coaching businesses I have… Confidence and empowerment.

Confidence to take the right steps forward to achieve results, to change your life, and the empowerment that equips you with the skills, knowledge and experience to continue growing and achieving for the rest of your life.

BONUS COACHING

The bonus coaching area you can sign up for free by getting this book is to give you the hand holding and coaching that gives you the simple step-by-step solution.

You get free access at: http://www.chrisdufey.com/100clientsbonus

With every business mentoring client I have, its my job to take a 'stake' in their success, if I show them and hand-hold them to doubling or tripling their clients, or 10x their profits, and then I let them go to continue… but in a years time, its all crumbled – I've failed as a coach.

Rather than me talking about the book to come, I've included feedback from the working draft. By having this you've been added to the VIP launch list of getting your hands on the book before it goes public, and also giving you access to a private forum where I can help and guide you, and you can also become apart of the creation of this book.

The title "Small Steps Big Business" is the working title. I gave it all about 60sec thought, and will do the headline testing in final stages before publishing, this is another part of the behind the scenes action you will see be becoming apart of the private group.

"Stop trading time for money, it's the worst trade in the world."
—Tont Robbins

INTRODUCTION

"It's a lie."

These exact three words going through my head as I speed down the main road of Dubai racing to get home in time.

I wasn't racing against the clock, I was racing to get home in time to give my daughter a bottle and put her to bed. I had been up since 4:30 am, my usual wake up time to give me enough time to shower, eat, read and be in the gym in time for my first client starting at 6:00am.

You and I have been lied to about the same thing. I started my own business with the dream of 'working my own hours,' 'earning great money,' and 'being my own boss.' All of this was the complete opposite of what was going on, as I spent the entire day in the "office" which for me being a personal trainer was the gym. And I didn't want to be a dad that was at work the whole time missing out on my children's lives.

To this very day of me writing this, I get emails and private messages from countless trainers, coaches, consultants, and business owners who are struggling to earn the income they want.

Does this sound familiar?

- "I can't get new clients, it's a constant battle of me chasing them, and I'm losing my love of why I got into this."
- "I feel like a sham when it comes to 'selling' my services."
- "The market is so flooded, I can't stand out."
- "Why are other coaches getting clients and making more money than me when they are less competent than I am, with fewer skills and credentials?"
- "I can't earn more money, I'm struggling to make ends meet, and I might have to go get a job."
- "I'm stuck in the time-for-money trap and have no more time to make the money that I want. My income is stuck."

It sounds familiar because these are the problems that we are lured into when following the mainstream, regurgitated advice when starting, growing and building a business that we run.

It doesn't have to be this way, and I wrote this book to give you the answers to ensure that these problems go away forever. Don't just read, but use this information to understand exactly how to build a business that can work without you slaving away at it. Even better, where you can disappear and come back to it, for it to be only growing stronger from when you left. And best yet, your bank account has grown in that time as well.

I've got the upper hand to see what's working, what's not, and what the absolute best strategies and tactics are to use for trainers, coaches, and consultants because they are my clients, and that's what I'm here to give you. Week to week, I get to delve deeply into how each client can deliver the best possible results for their own customers and clients, how they can grow a business that gives them the money, freedom, and lifestyle they want.

Ultimately… that's what you want, that's why you are here.

Happiness is a broad term and has as many meanings as people you ask, just like the word 'success.' I will show you later how to define and then make this happen for yourself.

Being a personal trainer and physique coach myself, I started out showing, then teaching and guiding other trainers how to grow their businesses simply because I got asked so many times "how have you done it?" or "how are you living in Bali running these businesses?" The emails came in so often, I decided I had to do something about it.

On a day by day basis I was seeing the lies that were being perpetuated on the web and social media. Business coaches were simply regurgitating what their business coach told them, to sell people a 'stairway to nowhere' program that would only leave their pockets empty and more frustrated in what to do.

I firmly stand against the 'theory only' and unproven tactics that only lead you to spinning your wheels, being busy and not achieving.

This book is for any type of trainer, coach, or consultant and I will boil down those terms to just 'coach' for ease for you throughout this book. As coaching is an efficient and high-impact means to get results with clients, coaching has grown to encompass many fields; business coaches, fitness coaches, life coaches, executive coaches, career coaches, sales coaches, and now the role of consultants such as marketing, interior design, dentists, lawyers, and the list goes on.

The same major problems and bottlenecks come up time and time again, which is when they come to me to quickly push down, move over or around, to then grow a business that leads to that all-consuming 'success.'

You have ahead of you the key steps to make serious changes to your business so that you can;

- Attract new clients each day and week. Even better, have them hunting you down and ready to pay a premium.
- Grow your income to double, triple, or even 10x what you are earning now by changing the business model so you can deliver world-class results to every client and leverage your time, resources, and profits.
- You charge what you are worth and have the system in place so that you turn someone that's interested into a client for the long-term and never be 'salesy.'
- You grow a team around you and have multiple income streams so you are never pigeon-holed or restricted with growth, being an exponential means to grow your success and income.

Coming up now is the 5-Key Steps for you to use to get these results:

Step 1: Your Foundation

The first moves someone takes after deciding to start their business and jump into being an entrepreneur is usually; what's my business name, what should my logo look like, and go get business cards printed up. This is all wrong.

Your future, success, and business all rely on the foundation and platform you set for it, and I will walk you through what really matters, and when you have finished using this, you will see how it literally impacts every other facet, decision, and part of your business.

Step 2: Marketing and Attracting New Clients

The words of sales and marketing have been ruined by mistruths and downright lies with how to go about and action these to build your business. These words now cross over in many aspects. The more effective your marketing, the easier and fewer steps there are in the sales process. Importantly this is an 'engine' that you can set up to run for you 24/7.

Waking up from a great sleep, whilst going for a run, being on holiday, or finishing dessert, and then you realise that you just had a new client come on board, sales have been made, and the cash is sitting in your account, or fresh new leads that equal both of those wins are now ready for your sales team to tackle. These are the fruits of simple, yet effective and powerful marketing can give you when done right.

Step 3: Converting New Clients

'Sales' is not a dirty word… being a salesman doesn't make you a bad person. The hang up so many people have when it comes time to talk sales, or to sell yourself to someone is hilarious. People don't buy something they don't want or need. Sales are simply connecting the dots for someone having a problem and getting delivered a solution.

You are always selling, whether it's your products or services, yourself, or your opinion in an everyday chat, it's all very similar. We are not going to go into dirty tactics of persuasion or unethical means to make a sale. Because there is no need. And I will show you how that also includes using the 'client pipeline' that ensures you take on only the perfect type of client that's willing to pay the premium but never feels like 'selling.'

Step 4: Delivering World Class Results

You can only sell crap once... Because once someone knows it's shit, they will never buy it again, and with the power of social media, now you can have the world know very easily and with speed just how bad your failing products and services are.

Instead, I will show you how to create the perfect 'signature system' that gets your clients the best results, and doesn't suck all of your and grows your profits. As you are in the results game, your clients are coming on board for results, and the benefit of paying a coach is to have – certainty.

The certainty is that they will get those results and have you hand-hold guide, and give them the advice needed to make that happen.

The truth is I have the 'red velvet rope' of a strategy consultation that will not just let anyone come on board my coaching programs. Because I only want to take on people that I like, that I believe in, and that are not energy vampires that will just waste both of our time.

Step 5: The Ultimate Profit Strategy Plan

These small steps are going to give you the big success you are looking for, but only if you use them and take action.

This is not a read once, and put back on the shelf book, this is a guide, along with the 'downloadable coaching' I have for you for buying this book. To ensure that you take the steps needed to achieve the business and lifestyle success you want..

I find most businesses fail because the owner is standing in the way of success. Not willing to think or do for what's needed. I will show you how to continually build your business for the money, freedom, and lifestyle you want.

With the 5-Key steps laid out for what's to come, it's a good question that I always ask when sitting in a course or presentation, reading a book, or listening to advice.... Does this person have the expertise to actually give out this information?

Sitting here in my Bali villa being able to run 4 companies, and having the true luxury of lifestyle design at my fingertips, it's not always been rainbows and lollipops for me. Far from it –

Being a personal trainer for over 10 years, I hit the wall of not being able to grind through another 60+ hour work week of seeing my clients. I knew I wanted more, more for my life, my wife, and my brand new baby girl at the time, and for the positive impact, I knew I could make to the world, wanting to truly help people live richer, happier lives.

There was only one reason I had grown myself to being a top personal trainer in Dubai, and before flying over, in Sydney. I sought out the best coaches, courses, and information the world had to offer, spending everything I had to soak in what would make me the best. Though, I then hit the roadkblack that my business needed to change, and drastically. I had to learn business.

So I did what I knew best, I went out and studied, learned, and soaked in the best information from the best people, from every industry to then apply it to growing my own businesses and now all of my clients and customers.

It slapped me across the face that I was having daily 'aha' moments of being blown away that we were living in Bali, and having the ability work on the projects and businesses I love. One of the biggest realisations early on was when, I at the beach with my girls when I got a message from my personal assistant. He had just finished the months reporting and from the coaching business I had started only 5 months before I had done over $100,000 in just that month.

What was a total dream for me just years ago, for what was a year's income I had just done in 1 month, in only 1 of my businesses. And the way that I look at it, money is just value, people will only exchange money for value, and that means I was delivering bucket loads more value to the world.

If you really read through and take action on what I have here for you, you are going to be able to create the income, freedom, and success that you truly want.

This isn't just some throwaway, pep talk comment. This is the truth as I have done it, and continue to do this with my clients all around the world. This is the 'system' that I know works.

If you wait to use this, put aside and say "I'll come back to it," then don't even bother reading ahead. You have to be ready to use this, to take head-on the roller-coaster that is being an entrepreneur and enjoy the ups and downs without ever stopping.

The only true reason I am in the position I am in now and am writing this for you, is because I never gave up. I failed far more times that I did things right, though it was from constantly correcting course, learning, and making adjustments that I continue to move towards what I want to achieve.

It's now your time to do it 10x faster and bigger than I did, by avoiding the mistakes and fast-tracking your success by using what works.

Don't Forget…

Join the Bonus area before continuing on so have the coaching videos, guides and templates to use everything I am about to take you through.

Get all-access by going to:
http://www.chrisdufey.com/100clientsbonus

ABOUT ME

Hi…

I'm Chris Dufey and I want to give you the exact steps I know to work, as they are proven by me going through it and now running 3 online businesses and living here in Bali with my wife and 2 young daughters. And also, coaching and mentoring trainers and coaches around the world to create their 'dream fitness business.'

There's a big problem with personal training that is the underbelly that no one wants to talk about… and I was stuck in it for years.

I ran a personal training business with multiple trainers working for me in Sydney, I even ran a PT business in Dubai and charging top dollar to even train top fitness models to Arab Sheiks. Though I was always stuck in the 'Time-for-Money' trap.

Selling your time means you are selling your most precious asset, and this also means that your success and how much money and freedom you can have is capped. You can only see a certain number of clients per day or per week as there are only a certain number of hours in the week.

I've done 70 hours of face-to-face training and consulting as a personal trainer… and it was hell! …and it was then the question struck me, "what if I could do something once, and get paid over and over for it."

Which means you are able to:

- Have the positive, life and body changing impact on so many more people. As we do what we do as trainers because we want to help people.
- Earn the money and the income you want.
- Live the lifestyle you want, as you have the freedom.

The freedom factor is a big one for me personally. I'm able to work from my home office, live anywhere we want in the world, and I work only on the projects I want, and I am very picky with the clients I take on board.

Being stuck in a gym, and knowing that if I don't see my clients, I don't earn money. Which meant anytime I wanted time off, go on holiday, or do something else, I was losing money. There was no long term security as it relied 100% on me having to be there, I just had a job that I ran myself.

This was when I first started down the path of creating my first online fitness business, which has now flourished. As being able to travel the world, speak on this very topic, and mentor others that want the success, I feel grateful that I can give this to you.

There is no doubt about it, that online fitness is a gigantic business. If you don't embrace it, you will be left behind… far, far behind.

And the ability to scale – which means you can impact and give value to so many more people and how powerful the new methods of getting you, your message, and your offer in front of your perfect audience is astounding.

It's as easy as ever to build a business that gives you what you want, yet the problem is there are so many people failing to do so. So many trainers, coaches, and fitness enthusiast are trying to build an online business and literally failing.

The only reason this is happening is that they are doing the wrong things. Following the wrong plan and getting lied to about the new hot fads with internet marketing.

You are reading this right now because you want more…

More money, freedom, and options in your life to do what you want and to have a bigger impact.

As to the point of me writing this for you, I was just overseas as a private mastermind with some very high-end entrepreneurs. Entrepreneurs that are running up to 8-figure businesses – Yes, that means they make over $10 million each year. The potential for you to make big money on the internet is real.

And making money is not a bad thing as this means you are giving value to the world. Adding real value and impacting people's lives for the better. And the reason why everyone has to apply to come on board my programs and coaching is because I have to make sure everyone is up to the right level to give great value to the world.

I don't want to help advocate or promote more crappy quality online fitness programs that just bring down the industry. I want to help the quality trainers and coaches that get results to create the business to impact their own lives.

So here it is…

You have the step-by-step guide to literally starting and growing your dream online fitness business right here.

The difference between the winners and the losers Is that the people who create their success and those that don't is action! Being able to focus on the few but very powerful actions that will give you the business success.

1 THE 3-SUCCESS FACTORS FOR YOUR (AND MY) ONLINE BUSINESS

Not long ago, I was having lunch with a friend who runs a successful online business and we got talking about how we got started in this. When we first met at the Old Man's, which is a great restaurant/bar at a beach here in Bali, we we're watching all the surfers and tourists do their thing.

They were walking slowly to and from the surf, others were sitting back and drinking beers and cocktails, and then there was us, having a lunch and we both had meetings to get to shortly after – this was still a work day, we weren't on holiday, though we still had the freedom to meet up in the middle of the day to catch up and chill out.

Even thinking back to when I was a personal trainer, I ran boot camp sessions for 3 days a week for 3 years straight. I was waking at 4:30 every morning, and it was so I had enough time to get started on the day to see my 6am clients. Trying to earn more money I did more sessions, at one point I was seeing 70 hours' worth of consultations and training sessions in a week.

It was not worth it!

At the end of those weeks, I was fried, there was no way that losing all my energy, time for my girlfriend, social life, and even time for me and my training was worth a few extra dollars. That was not living, that was dying.

I got smarter at one point and brought on trainers to work for me. This was great, and it flourished into a full personal training agency where I had a team of trainers working for me throughout Sydney. This is why I'm still very much a fan of a location or 'bricks-and-mortar' business, however even local businesses need to leverage the power of online marketing and platforms available these days.

It was when I was in Dubai that I had a full book of personal training clients within weeks of landing. When I first moved there, I had only a few months to get the business running, life sorted in a whole new country, and ready for my wife and brand new baby girl that would be born soon.

This was when I started 'dipping my toe in' and learning about online marketing as I knew it was the way forward and would give me the leverage and power to create the business success and future that I had been working so hard to get to. Literally learning from everything I could, I was engrossed with finding out how it all works and what was needed to be done.

I found that it started coming together, and by learning from the right resources, and finding the right mentors I was now bringing in more leads than I could handle for my personal training. This is where I decided to start my online personal training business and focus on growing this. It was the nagging thought that kept popping up for so long that I wanted the freedom to not be stuck in a gym, to be able to live around the world, to earn the money that gave me financial freedom, and to start living the lifestyle that I really wanted.

When I first started my online personal training, I was picking up clients and doing everything I could to give them the best experience and results possible. Literally pouring everything in that I had learnt over 10 years of personal training and the countless courses and certification I had attained.

Then I knew the power of selling programs and products online where it could sell 24/7 and not have me manually spend time delivering it, total automation. And this was the step I needed for the freedom factor I was looking for.

When I launched my first product, I had the payment processor with PayPal, and the app was on my phone. So it notified me whenever a payment would come through.

I remember carefully clicking the final buttons to launch the program and sending off the list I had built up so far. Was it going to completely crash and burn, or was it going to work? I could only wait as it was late at night and I had to go to bed to wake up early for my clients the next day.

This whole process was done in the home office I had created in our spare bedroom, and I was not staring out over the famous Palm Jumeriah in Dubai as our apartment was right in the middle of it.

I woke up the next morning, turned my phone on, and there it was. The constant buzz of the PayPal app going off with new payments coming through. I couldn't believe that I was sitting in my lounge room having breakfast, and I was earning money.

Later that day myself, my wife Lauren, and my daughter Arlo were driving to have lunch, and there it was, still going off every now and then. I was just spending time with my family, going out for lunch, and I was earning money. Compare that to just having to be in the gym to see my clients, where the stress if I was ever sick, went on holiday, or wasn't able to get to the gym, I wouldn't earn any money.

Now sitting next to the beach here in Bali, chatting about how I got started and the tough times of learning, failing, and finding a way through to where we were now, I look back at 3 major things that I had done that made all this possible.

These 3 factors are what I show my members and clients straight away, along with the steps on how to use them and connect them with what's needed for them to go from where they are now to the business success they want in the shortest possible time.

#1 - Grow Your Following

I hear it all the time. A trainer, coach, or budding entrepreneur has the idea of the perfect program, service, or product. There is a big flaw with people thinking that ideas are worth a lot of money... The problem is that it's a lie.

Most people get started by trying to find the perfect business name, getting their logo done, having a pretty website put together showcasing who they are, business cards getting printed up... and on it goes.

Today, the power is at your fingertips, and the ability to reach your perfect audience has never been so easy.

You need to grow a following, a group of raving fans first, and you do that by putting great value out there to help people.

Through a basic website, that yes, it needs to look good, but the one aim of it is to get people to consume the great free value that you are giving away. And of course, we have to mention social media, as this is a must for everyone to leverage.

You should never ask something of someone before you give first. This is why, by giving out great value and helping people with their specific problems that you are the specialist at, you are getting people to know you, like you, and trust you.

Too many people are solely focused on what I call 'vanity metrics,' which is how many likes or followers someone has on their social media platforms. Where time and time again, I see that the size of your following does not equal business success. There are steps in-between to rocket your business and profits.

With social media, it's to build relationships and ultimately also take them off that social media platform and build an email list with it. This means you can use the power of email to continue building the relationships and giving value away.

Let me give you a great example of a trainer, Mark, who has just gone through this in my program.

Literally starting with zero online assets, Mark had no following on social media, no website, no email list, nothing. When Mark came to me, he wanted to have a thriving online business. He was worried about if it was able to happen as he had none of the online 'stuff' or 'tech' know-how.

He soon learned that this was not a problem. After going through a clarity session, and doing a message-market-media match, he was clear on what his uniqueness was that separated him from the rest of his competitors in the saturated weight-loss market for men. He knew now in depth his target market, and where he would best be able to put his marketing message to get in front of them.

His aim was to produce articles covering certain topics he now knew that his target market wanted to know more about, and he could give the guides, advice, and plans to help them solve their specific issues. Producing this through a starting website that was created in just 2 weeks, his aim was to first engage them through Facebook, build his Facebook following, and then also have a lead magnet to drive them off into his email list.

His email marketing strategy was very simple, it was just 3 series of emails, that would, 80% of the time, just give away free value. Using the rest of it, he was able to promote his coaching program.

Within a few short months, everything was running smoothly, and both his social media following was growing, but also importantly, his email list was growing as well, and new clients were steadily coming on board each week.

The aim here that I took Mark through, and with 95% of my clients, is to grow a strong following first, as you are able to leverage this into so much more. This is also important as they are going to give you the feedback needed to help you make the right decisions.

Things such as what programs to create, what's involved in your programs, how do you best deliver it, what topics do you create content on...and so much more. This is where you can directly reach out and have them give you the answers.

You will even find that in the very first email when a person signs up to all my online businesses, I am asking them to reply back to me with an answer to one question. The one question I ask is different each time depending on why they signed up, and for what business. However, these answers are gold to my business. They give me the direct insights into how I best serve them.

#2 – The Offer/Value Seesaw:

Coming from the personal trainer world, there are so many people that think, "I'm not a salesman, I'm a trainer, so I don't know how, or shouldn't be selling."

This is a complete lie, no matter what you do, everyone is selling something. You are selling the restaurant where you want to go for dinner to your friends, you're selling yourself at a job interview, you're selling yourself to pick up a date, etc.

When you are running your own business, it's your job to sell as best as possible. If you are truly good at what you do, you get results for your clients, and it is your duty to the world and the people that have the problems that you solve to get your services, programs, and products in their hands.

A big question when it comes to selling is, "how often, or how hard do I push?" This is a legitimate question, especially when talking about social media it can be, "how many posts should be selling my program?" or about email marketing it can be, "how many sales emails should I send?" I go by a simple rule and have laid this out in an easy to use a process that works.

The 80/20 rule of value to offers. In his great book, Jab Jab Jab Right Hook, Gary Vaynerchuck shows you with specific examples how you need to offer great value numerous times, and then you can put your offer out there. If you are pushing too hard and too often, people will get turned off, and stop following you.

Though, if you're not offering enough, you're leaving a lot of money on the table. And the people that are hot potential customers don't get the opportunity for coming on board.

This means that 80% of the time, my focus is to deliver nothing but great value. To give content that my markets can consume and use and get results from. This also means that the value and the offers that you are crafting are truly made for your market. And this is where combining a message-market-media match and especially knowing what your 'uniqueness' is that separates you from your competitors is so important.

If you know your market well enough, you can create the exact content that they value and crave for more of. This is where phenomenal content is king, as out in the big wide world of the internet it's thick with 'average.'

The other 20% of the time, you are to sell, promote, and give your offer to the right people. And you are not to pussy-foot around with it either. I've had numerous trainers come on board my coaching that have already been trying to build their online business, and when I go deep diving into how they are running everything, there are huge gaps in their promoting what their business does.

They are breaking a cardinal rule; "make it easy to buy." I will go through this in more detail soon, and you will see how easy it is to have the natural set of steps of takes someone that doesn't know you, to your clients.

#3 - Working with a mentor

I believe in personal training and coaching. If someone wants to get in great shape, improve their performance or health, and feel great about themselves, the well-designed physical training and proper nutrition programs are bases for us all thriving at life.

"When the student is ready, the teacher will appear"... this is a quote that I think is so true. I always think it when I pick up a new book and start reading. Even if I'm reading a book that I've already read before. New things are jumping out at me, new ideas are flooding into my head, and it's like I've picked this book up at the exact right time for solving problems and growing improvement at the time that I need them.

When I first started my online business in Dubai, I was soaking up everything I could. From podcasts to videos, to books, guides, the lot. Every spare second was devoted to trying to learn more and then put it into action. I wanted to become one of the best and was obsessed with getting out of my position of being stuck in a gym, and getting to the freedom of running my online business.

Things were progressing at first, step by step it was growing, my list and following was increasing, and sales were trickling in. But not at the rate it needed to or that I wanted it at for me to have the 'success' I had in my mind.

There is only so far you can go on the self-help route, and when I was thinking just like when I was competing in sports, at the time I was prepping for a physique show, I had a coach writing my plans and programs. I had coaches asking me why I had a coach when I was a physique coach myself, and the answer is it's about having the outside perspective and accountability that adds jet fuel to the fire.

If Michael Jordan and Tiger Woods have a coach, and Richard Branson has a host of advisors, then if I want to excel I need a mentor and someone that has been there, and has the experience to show me the steps to follow.

This is exactly why I wanted to start showing and coaching others for their business success. As I had such a great improvement in so many areas of my life, I want to share this and give this to others.

I went and found a business coach and mentor that literally step-by-step took me through everything I was doing wrong that I could fix, he showed me how to set my business up, and what I needed to be working on that really mattered to really excel my results.

So many times, it's so easy for us to get caught up with just being 'busy.' But the truth is, being busy does not equal being productive, and getting done what's going to propel your business forward. Working 40 hours a week only proves that you have worked 40 hours a week, nothing more.

Without my coach, I wouldn't have learned the importance and skills of writing ad copy that sells or building my traffic and plugging the holes where I was losing traffic, or even the best ways to create a professional product and how to sell it.

In a matter of months, I had the 'leap frog' effect of taking huge jumps in all areas of my business that has now gotten me to where I am today. And this is why I wanted to create this program for you. To give you a powerful start, and a plan to follow for you to create the financial independence and freedom.

I look forward to helping you reach all your goals.

2 CLARITY

Why do you get up in the morning?

Bering able to wake up with a strong passion, determination, and focus on what you are going to achieve in the day is one of the most powerful factors that will have you achieving what you want.

But, time and time again, the biggest problem is that you don't 'truly' know what you want. And therefore, you will never really achieve what you want.

Not only is your vision and purpose critical to yourself, but it's also critical to your business, so you are able to stand head and shoulders above your competition. Your market, your potential customers, and clients need to be lead, they need to know why you are doing what you do first.

Knowing why over what you do will ultimately create the following you need.

Can you easily explain and articulate in a short burst of words what you do, what you're offering, and get people to buy into your visions and they know that you are the answer for them?

This is one of the most important factors that I will walk you through very soon as this will affect how you attract new clients, to how you deliver results for them. The issue you need to overcome here is that most people are ranting and raving about 'what' they do. Talking about all the technical features of what they offer or how they do the work they do. Then others talk about the "how" which is the process that sets them apart. A better next steps is to understand and share the message of 'why' you do what you do. So that it truly engages emotions and you can lead people in the right direction.

This simply boils down to, the difference between these two statements

- "I'm a personal trainer" – (the What)
- "I help people transform their bodies and health giving them greater happiness" – (the Why)

Which of these two statements do you like more? Which one do you think latches onto and helps bring someone around to at least knowing more about you?

Your goal is to create a clear outlook of what you want to achieve, and then know the why. As people don't buy what you do, they buy why you do it. When using this in your marketing and your copy along with the messages you're sending out, being able to easily communicate the value (aka the "why") will trigger intrigue, and move them along to becoming a client.

Ultimately people only want to know what can you do for them. Not caring about the certifications you have as much as you do. But what is even more powerful is being able to show them that you can solve the problems they have and that you do what you do for the right reasons. The truth is, everyone is sceptical, even with this book I'm sure you had hesitations. You would have asked yourself, why should I invest my time and money in this? Is it worth it?

If you've seen the videos, read the articles, or listened to the podcasts that I have produced, my two main objectives are to 1) give our great value that you can apply and 2) build a community and a relationship with everyone in that community. My message and what my 'why' is something I make sure I share out. And sure, this means that a lot of people won't be into what I do, and I'm perfectly alright with that. The powerful part is that if you do vibe, and agree with where I am. My very first purpose of giving out and sharing real value that will help you will bring you into my community.

There is no doubt that you need to have a clear vision of what you need to create, and that's what I'm going to help you create. A part of what you want to create comes into the money and financial part of your life.

Money is not the be all and end all, and I learned that while living in Dubai and being close to extreme wealth and knowing they were not happy. I'm not going to lie, money is still an important slice of the pie in your success, happiness, and lifestyle.

So how much money do you want to earn?

$100,000 a year, $1million a year, or why not $10million a year?

The truth is you've probably got a random number in your head that you think once you have, then all your problems will disappear, and you'll live life with a constant smile. Or, you're being more modest and just want to be comfortable.

It all boils down to what you really want, and it's why I've included in the downloadable success sheets how to find out how much money you really want to earn. By going through and creating your ideal lifestyle expenses, really mapping out how much it will cost you to buy the things you want, live the lifestyle you want, travel, eat, charity, save, cars, homes, education, and everything else… You will finally know the number that will at last bring you to living the life you want.

Once you reach that, you can always re-evaluate, and I recommend you do reassess, though the point is to set a firm target, and make that happen. For every client that comes on board, myself or my team ask, 'What's your goal income, how much money do you want to make?"

We ask this because if you want to make $100,000 a year, or $2 million a year, the business that is going to give you this is different. On some aspects, it can be very similar, though we want to avoid having bottlenecks and problems arising that will flat-out stop you in your tracks.

For example, let's use a personal trainer and the usual selling his time. Let's call this personal trainer Mark.

Mark sells hour-long personal training sessions, once he's got all his lead attractions strategies working, he can convert them into new clients, and he's got 40 hours of booked sessions each week. Mark charges, $80 an hour and he's bringing in $3,200 each week.

This example has Mark doing very well by normal standards. Though there are serious problems at hand that so many in his position and industry, forget to think about. Paying taxes, the wavering inconsistency of client's sessions, him being stuck to that location to service his clients, the amount of back-end work needed to service these clients, and still try to build the business in other avenues.

Mark is working around the clock to handle this, and can easily reach burn-out and full-on fatigue. The issue still arises that he'\s only making just over $150,000, and that's before tax, so be ready to take a chunk out of that. If Mark's goal is to earn $500,000 a year, it can never happen with this model.

He can't do three times the amount of work he is doing, its impossible. So therefore, the entire business model has to change. And the blaringly obvious problem is that it's not just personal trainers that have this problem, all coaches and consultants that 'sell time' will reach these issues.

This is why I'm going to show you how to expand your business and success ceiling later in this book, but before I do, and before you can, there are some key steps I am going to walk you through. The number-one biggest problem I see with all business owners is the lack of clarity on what they want to achieve.

I'm not an advocate of really knowing the exact clear outcome for your 10-year plan or beyond. That can be too daunting, and I also believe unrealistic, as we are always taking twists and turns. I even hope that after you read this book, that your beliefs and what you know is possible have expanded, and that you strive to achieve more. This is something that I see with every single client and member, as the very first coaching call and in the first phase we work on clarity, though for me to really outline what needs to be, I have to know what they want to achieve. After the first 3 to 4 months, the goal always explodes to become bigger. Their minds are open to what is really capable of happening, and the limiting beliefs and small thinking they suffered from before have been washed away.

This is why I want you to create the outline of what you want to achieve in 1 year, and then at the end of this book, with the coaching in the downloads, you will map out a 12-week phase. I don't really plan any further than 1 quarter ahead. This way I can outline what I want to achieve, and work out what steps need to be made, what actions I need to make on a day by day scale. This way there is no overwhelming, it's quite literally following a map. And that's what I want to give you with this book.

Success comes in multiple currencies, and I see financial success as just one slice of the pie. Living and working in Dubai, I was surrounded by immense wealth and had the pleasure of coaching and living around some extremely wealthy individuals. Though many were not the happiest around. Polarising that to when I backpacked around South America with my now wife, our first stop was Chile, which is where my mother and her family is from. I had the pleasure of spending time with my great grandmother in a tiny little village south of Santiago.

The village population was tiny, everything was walking distance from each other, and there was no real money, everyone bartered what they had for something else. We traded corn for freshly made cheese that morning or for a bottle of milk, the tomatoes for bread, and on it went. Everyone seemed so much happier, and them just knowing I was a distant relative from another country were more than happy to give me the clothes off their back.

The point is that money does matter, and I won't make a song and dance how it's not because I am driven and want material things, I love living the quality lifestyle I do, though it's not the be all and end all.

What you have to answer to design your business to give you exactly what you want starts with four questions.

What do you want to do?
When do you want to do it?
Where do you want to do it?
Whom do you want to do it with?
And, why do you do it?

These are extremely powerful questions, as I know when I first gave them the respect they deserved and answered these and then acted upon them. Design your business and life so that you are doing what you love, what you deliver the most value with and what brings you to your major goals. You should decide when you want to do it. Does this involve finishing work by 2pm each day? This is what I decided and what I do. Then comes to where you want to do it, as for me, I wanted the freedom and independence to be able to live and work anywhere in the world that myself and my family wanted. I'm writing this for you now in Bali, I know some later chapters will be written in other countries as we do some travelling and take time off.

And then importantly, it's deciding who you want to surround yourself with and work with. As for developing a team, and who is a part of your business, you need to bring on the best. The right people, united together can steer a business to success with the right vision. As I know you probably only have a very small team, or maybe it's just you, the question is, "who do you surround yourself with?"

This is so important I can't just let you glaze over it, and there are more strategies later that will touch upon this as this is one of the most powerful things you can do for your business success. The people you are around need to bring you up, give you positivity, give you honest feedback, and help you when needed. As a coach, I see it a pivotal role being to pat my clients on the back for a job well done, and give a gentle and swift kick up the backside when they are not living up to their own expectations. This is because we all slow down, fall into a hump, and get distracted. So we need the people around us to drive us forward, inspire us, and improve our lives.

When you cover those four questions, and I highly recommend you do it today with the worksheets I have for you, then you are in the position to truly design the business and life you want to live.

3 BEING BUSY VS. ACHIEVING

What's the usual response to someone when asked, "How are you going?" It's usually a brief and overlooked, "OK" following up with an "I'm so busy."

It's almost a patch of honour to be working day and night, toiling away at your work, and now the fad is the 'hustle.' The common problem I see time and time again is that there is very little, or nothing, actually being achieved. The end goal isn't getting closer, and what's going on is just being busy for the sake of being busy.

Ticking off your to-do items gives you a dopamine rush, it makes you feel good, and I will put my hand up first to say that I fell into this trap by just doing meaningless tasks and not sinking my teeth into the real meat that was going to make the business grow and income pour in.

It's time to drop glorification of busy, as there are no bonus points for being exhausted, stressed, and just doing things. Though the problem is we have to bust another lie right now, and that is about multi-tasking.

Multi-tasking is not the answer to getting more done and achieving what you want. Your focus is one of the most precious assets you have, and if you are throwing it away by juggling tasks in the hope to build your business, you're doomed. I know all too well with the need to try and multi-task, I run 4 companies, and I have to slap myself out of it when trying to handle different tasks for different businesses, as the end result is never great, and that's what we need to produce – greatness.

You can still have variety, it only means that while you are working on a particular task, for that duration of time, you work on that task and that task alone. Especially not hopping around from Facebook to emails, to text messages, you need to switch it all off and get what you need to get done.

One of the most important tactics you can use is implementing the Most Important Tasks (MITs) for each day. This is where you identify exactly what the number one, two and three most important tasks of that day are that need to be accomplished.

I always like to boil it down to the major MIT for the day. Start with the one thing, and knock this off first for the day. The MIT that is usually the hairiest, and scariest thing you want to do, usually gets procrastinated about, and you start doing other less important tasks that keep your ego happy by thinking you are being busy. This number one MIT for each day needs to be goal orientated and a clear next step that needs to be done for you to move closer to your goal.

The key for this is to do this as the very first piece of work you do each day. I don't even look at social media, emails, or anything else until this number one MIT is completed. It's a part of my morning routine, where by 8pm at the latest, I've already ticked off the biggest task for the day.

The other curve ball I am going to throw you now is the question, "does it need to be done, and does it need to be done by you?" This question gets you thinking on another level, where most coaches are stuck in the day to day grind, you can catapult yourself ahead of your competition by thinking like a real business person. Firstly, is the task actually needed to be done, or done now, opens up the answer of what do you need to be working on right now. Then asking does it need to be done by you, opens the possibility that these are tasks that you should have team members that can easily be outsourced to contractors for.

My eyes were opened to this when I attended a mastermind in Bangkok. After spending 5 minutes explaining my businesses, my grand plan, and the issues I was facing to take it to the next level, I was asked how many team members I had. At the time, I had one full-time and 4 contractors in place. My mastermind colleagues and even I had it dawn upon us that everything was running too lean. So after some serious thinking, I took the leap, I decided to bring on 3 coaches. I would pay for them to live here in Bali with me, for me to mentor them, but also for them to work in my business. Then I started hiring other staff that were located around the world.

Now I appreciate you might not be in the position to do this yet, and that's perfectly OK, though I want you to see that you should not be doing everything, and the thinking that only you can do the job is actually sabotaging your business success. You have to get out of your own way and build a business that will grow without you slaving away.

Actioning, delegating, and deleting – these are the three decisions I make when looking at tasks. Do I do it myself and when do I give it to my team and create a system for it to be done repeatedly with effectiveness, or do we delete it and not do it.

This chapter is to get you to see the truth and to stop you getting to the end of each day and thinking, "I was busy all day, but what did I accomplish?" Because, as I outline and give you the steps to follow, the most important part is for you to actually follow it. Not only is this book going to give you the platform to build your coaching business, but it's also going to turn you into a greater entrepreneur.

This is exactly like a weight-loss client, and something I'm all too familiar with. I can write you a world-class diet, training program, and protocol that can take into account your metabolism, hormonal environment, previous history, and using information from blood, urine, and saliva testing, even delving into genetic testing. The problem is if you don't follow the plan, the plan is useless.

This is the truth with being a coach, and I'm here now as your coach. I need to open your eyes, stretch your beliefs and help you take action. Just like with any client, you pat them on the back for great work, and you give them a polite and swift kick up the backside when needed to get them moving in the right direction.

At the end of the day you want to be happy, and that encompasses your own definition of business success as well. Financial success and earning money are just two of the currencies of success, though if you're like me, you want to have a great lifestyle that's filled with freedom. Your work-life balance is one of the parts of this machine we call life, and I don't think it's necessarily looked at the right way by most people.

I see things come and go in seasons when there is a new business starting, campaigns launching, or big next steps to come, there is a season where I will be working more hours and more focused on specific tasks. Before I finished writing this book, I was collapsing 4 of my businesses into 2. To do this the right way, and the way that I knew would grow the business short and long term, this involved a huge content audit that included over 140 podcasts episodes and 120 videos that needed to be re-edited, and I don't even know how many blog posts.

Granted I had a team working on this, and I had to lead them through it, ensuring everything was done as needed and also on time. As like so many things, certain tasks can't be started until others are completed, so making sure all the dominos are lined up correctly to tip them over is only part of the job. Making sure that everything is working smoothly and in sync with each other meant I got to a point that I needed to take a break from writing the book. My focus had to go into the content production and editing of the two business's and making sure that once it's set up, it can organically grow with just needing a small amount of work. Once all this was done it gave me the opportunity to entirely jump into the book with no distractions.

One of the main aims of the book, with my members, clients, and with myself is to be solely focused on taking action on only what really counts. There is too much of the time that you are getting caught up with tasks, jobs, and sucked into responsibilities that you shouldn't be. I designed this entire book to walk you through the critical steps, and in the right order so that you can take action after each step, then finally at the end have everything together to be constantly acting on.

Yes, at the beginning, and when getting your business off the ground, you are going to be wearing many different hats, and being a generalist when it comes to what you have to do. You as the business owner and leader, the entrepreneur, means you only have very few major tasks that you need to focus on to propel the business forward. I'm going to show you through the following chapters what they need to be, and how this will change from person to person as you are unique and have certain strengths and passions that you want to embrace.

4 POWER OF HABITS

"We are what we repeatedly do,
excellence then, is not an act, but a habit"
—Aristotle

We touched upon it in the previous chapter, but now it's time to delve head first into it.

Your actions are what produce your results, and your results are your success, and your actions are determined by your habits. So we can then say your success comes through your habits.

Do you have habits of success set in place?

We are habitual creatures, the same actions, the same thoughts all go on repeatedly each day. I was first truly fascinated with the science of habits when it came to how I can help people get in better shape and health. Why would someone double their calories, sugar, and fat intake in the last 15 minutes of the day by caving in and devouring a whole block of chocolate? Was it a physiological problem, or was it psychological?!

The answer to that question is that it can be both. I became good at being able to quickly change what was needed for clients to burn fat faster by not having those problems. Though, I saw that when some of my business coaching clients were having slow progression or hitting plateaus, I had to dig deep to find the answers, and it quickly came up that it was from them not taking the right actions.

I get asked numerous times, "how do I get so much done?" and the answer is simply I'm effective and efficient with my time. To me, if I am wasting time on useless things that are not driving me forward to my goals, I'm stealing from my wife and daughters. That's honestly how I see it. I could be doing something to achieve better business success, or spending quality time with my family. And if I'm wasting away my time on being ineffective, my family is losing out because of that.

The big lie that surrounds habits is that it does not take 21days to form one. The actual length of time differs with multiple factors and can be far longer, though the goal isn't to focus on how many days you have to get through doing it. Reaching an imaginary number of days is not how you get results.

There are great books and resources on habits, but I'm going to distil and give you some major fire power in making this work for you now, and also by using the downloadable success sheets, I will be able to guide you through the steps needed to truly get great results.

Motivation is tied in closely with goals and the habits you plan to form to achieve them. And I say 'plan' as you can start out with the right intention, but I am here to make sure they actually happen.

One of the best ways to do this is to set macro and micro quotas.

Setting big, hairy audacious goals is a great task that you need to do to shoot for bigger achievements. Though many people and this could be you, get daunted when looking at a big goal as there is so much involved in making this happen. Rather than telling you to "man up and own it," a smarter approach is to break the big goals into micro quotas.

You now know the breakdown of what smaller achievements you have to make to get there and these small quotas tie perfectly into what science is showing is real.

Consider this excerpt from Stanford psychologist B.J. Fogg on how he started his flossing habit:

"For me, cracking the code on flossing was to put the floss right by the toothbrush, and to commit to myself that I would floss one tooth — only one tooth — every time after I brushed.

I could floss them all if I wanted to, but the commitment was just one tooth.
[This works] because I was training the behavior. Maybe once every few weeks, I'd only actually floss one tooth, but a majority of the time I'd end up flossing them all."

Professor Fogg's entire system on *Tiny Habits* is built around the principle that it's better to set micro quotas to get out of the analysis phase and right into the action.

Now there is one step that separates the achievements of people that think about the goals they want to achieve, from the people succeeding at those.

At the moment, you're focused on the outcome of your goals, but that's not what you need to be thinking about.

This brings about the concept of behaviour-based goals and focussing on what are the key actions you need to continue doing that will eventually get you to where you want to go, you need only to focus on what behaviours and constant actions you need to do. Let's use the example of you wanting to lose 15kgs. Now just focussing on losing 15kgs isn't going to achieve any results except for when you jump on the scale and don't see the results you want.

If you focus on sticking to eating 5 wholefood, nutritious meals a day, and exercising each day, these are the behaviours that you need to make it happen.

For your business success, it could be that you spend the first 90 minutes of every day uninterruptedly working on your number on most important task. Rather than just thinking you want to make $250,000 this year.

The difference between outcome-based goals and behaviour based goals is night and day when it comes to fast-tracking your success. So the process is simple, and I have outlined it for you in the success sheets.

Your job now is to clearly outline what goals on macro and micro levels you want to achieve, and to be crystal clear on those and then break these down into the key behaviours you need to follow on a daily and weekly schedule.

5 TIME FOR MONEY TRAP

This is where we unveil a serious problem with your business and breaking through the ceiling to your success, though the issue is you're in the dilemma because everyone is. We just copied the same business model the same way that others were doing it and never thought there could be another way.

You are in the time-for-money trap, and this is what's stopping you from scaling your business to earn you the great money you want, stopping you from having freedom and living the lifestyle you want, and stopping you from having the high amounts of success that you set out to have in the beginning.

Not only are you being held down with this problem, but your ability to help more people in this world is capped. Grant Cardone in his many books I recommend says, "its your ethical responsibility to work for success". I agree, and I would also add if you have the skills and solution to others problems to do the best job you can in getting that out to the people that want it.

Coaches, consultants, speakers, freelancers... all are in the same boat of working for the time they put in. The lure of this problem is the hourly charge or wage you can have can be quite attractive, especially when starting out. It can bring you to a much higher than average level of income – but you and I are not here to be average. And that lure can be a cage made from gold, but at the end of the day, it's still a cage that's holding you back from going out and achieving more.

If you're like me, and one reason you picked up this book in the first place are finding yourself day dreaming of walking away from your business for a while, going on an extended holiday, going to live in other parts of the world, having a sabbatical, going to work on some other passion projects, and still having money come into the bank account, and better yet, have the business grow.

This I call an 'owner absent lifestyle business' and it's certainly an attractive dream, that far too often gets shut down when the thought 'I can never make this happen" pops up. You're not sure how to scale your business outside the bounds of trading more time, or possibly, the same time for money.

This book is designed to take you through the very important and very powerful first phase that I use with my clients. That is giving you a business that can scale, that has clients and customers coming to you, and being able to convert them into premium, long lasting, even recurring models of payments for you and your business.

There are a number of ways to earn more money in your business:

1. Increase charge amount per unit, for example, increasing your hourly rate.
2. Increase payment frequency, for example, the client can see you more often.
3. Increase revenue streams are the other services or products that will complement the business and solutions for the

client.

Over the next chapters, you will see how all of the above three can be done with ease once the right set-up is in place, but even before we get there, we want to look at two other options that will grow your business.

You need to use a more leveraged business model, and you need to build a team and outsource. Firstly with the outsourcing, we will cover that later, though don't get scared off for now if you don't think you're at the level to be able to do this, I will walk you through how to easily give the right tasks off so that you can concentrate on only what you are good at.

As you have been toiling and grinding away in the business for so long now, you have been wearing many hats, doing all the jobs. You simply need to find out what are the few keys tasks you are good at, and that you need to focus on that will bring the best results.

This comes to the thought of 'effective hourly rate' (EHR) that James Schramko taught me, and completely flipped my world upside down.

Let's use the example of the personal trainer again and say Courtney is a trainer that has 30 hours of sessions booked each week. If she is charging $80 an hour for those sessions, she will bring in $2,400 each week before tax and all other out-goings, but let's not even worry about that for now.

Courtney is pretty happy in thinking she takes in $2,400 each week, but the issue is that there are all the tasks outside of those sessions to run the business. Such as client upkeep that can involve writing diets, programs, check-ins, messaging, and emails. Then dealing with accounts, administrative tasks, the amount of time spent on social media, and this doesn't go into what we will cover later with using such strategies as content marketing to grow a strong following and new client funnel.

All this works equates to another 30 hours a week, so her effective hourly rate has now dropped to $40 an hour with the actual amount of work needed to earn that money has doubled.

This doesn't even take into the account the up and down of clients coming and going, not showing up, or being away that directly affect your money on a week to week basis.

When combining this concept with the 80/20 rule, you can break your tasks down into jobs earning you different amounts. Such as $10 an hour jobs would be data entry, tracking, admin tasks and social media posting. You have $100 an hour jobs that can be replying to emails and consultations. You have $1000 an hour jobs that can be creating high-grade content, developing sales copy, and delivering one-to-many coaching programs. Then you have $10,000 an hour jobs which would be marketing strategy design, sales, and marketing campaign development, and creating systems for team members to execute. You as the business owner need to take responsibility and ownership to focus on the higher end of what will propel the business and profits forward.

The solution first starts with knowing the problems your marketing is having on an intimate level, and why, in the next chapter, I walk you through exactly how to know this, and how to craft your business around delivering the perfect product, program, or service (or all three).

6 YOUR UNIQUENESS

What separates you from all of your competition, from your entire industry?

Why would someone happily pull out their wallet and hand over their hard-earned cash?

One of the most common questions I get is, "how do I make myself or my business unique?"

In marketing speak, this is known as the unique selling proposition or USP. Though before I show you how to create this for you and your business, there are two questions that you must ask yourself, and I'm here to show you how to get the answers so you are to be known as the 'go-to' person.

A USP is a way of summarising and telegraphing one of the chief benefits of the business or service being marketed.

A famous example of an effective USP that launched an empire of a business is, "fresh, hot pizza delivered in 30 minutes or less, guaranteed." Two major benefits that are specific are being expressed here in a short sentence. This example comes from the company

Dominos, and it is how it launched itself into a very competitive market.

The difference that you face in delivering a service is that you deal with intangibles, whereby a product-based business deals with tangibles. Generally, it's easier and simpler to convey value in marketing tangibles than intangibles. This is where productized service can be valuable, and why I will cover this for you coming up.

We have to start firstly at what I mentioned just before – your target market. Who are the exact type of people, the niche that you want to work in and become like a mini-celebrity for? All too often, we as business owners get so wrapped up in what we do, and fall in love with our product and service, that we lose sight of the results it brings and who it is for.

In the success sheets, I have the steps for you to identify your target market, and a powerful way to go about this and to also perfect what and how you run your business from a starting step is to survey your current clients.

A Unique Selling Proposition (USP) is one of the fundamental pieces of any solid marketing campaign. Simply stated, it's a summary of what makes your business unique and valuable to your target market. It answers the question: How do your business services benefit your clients better than anyone else can?

You have to step into the shoes of your potential clients' to see from their viewpoint how you can best serve them, and what they want. "Why should I buy from you?" – This is exactly the question you have to ask by standing in your potential clients' shoes, as they honestly have countless of other options.

It's not about the being the best, absolutely you want a great product and service, though it's not enough to make your business stand out. The real answer is that you don't want to compete at all, and by following the below 6 steps, you can clear away the competition and have clients coming to you.

If the word 'selling' puts you off, don't be scared, this is simply about differentiation, and truthfully, you are always selling yourself, whether it's for what restaurant you want to go to tonight, to your opinion of a TV show, to your success and livelihood.

There are an easy 6 steps you can follow to creating your USP.

#1 - Define your target market

Before you can start marketing your services, or even creating the 'how' you are going to deliver results, you need to know your target market, and this is why I walked you through the importance of this before, with one tactic of learning how already.

For example, you're not just a personal trainer that specializes in weight loss. You specialized in losing stubborn fat for middle-aged women.

This is so powerful to hone in on, because it changes your marketing, the language you use, and even how you create and develop your services and products to get the outcome your clients want.

You can see this is so powerful when you compare what a middle-aged woman wanting to lose some stubborn fat is looking for, compared to a 20-something male bodybuilder that wants to get huge and jacked. The way you would speak to those people, in being able to communicate that you are the right trainer for them is completely different.

Don't be afraid that you will be 'losing' clients by not focusing on them. You have to think of the upside, and the truth is, you are now going to attract so many more clients because it is crystal clear who it is you are a perfect fit for.

You have to be magnetic towards the right people and repulsive towards the wrong people.

Not that you go out of your way to repulse people that don't fit your target market, they just won't be interested, and glaze over like the example I gave above.

#2 – Define the problem you solve

Outline, spend the time and create clear communication of the problem you solve and be in the potential client's viewpoint.

Do you just help them lose weight? Or do you provide personalized diet and training coaching with a guarantee to lose weight or their money back? You can see that this slight change makes the impact so more powerful.

#3 – List the major benefits

Everyone gets wrapped up in the 'features' of what they do and all the ways they go about getting results for their clients. From the client's perspective, they don't really care. They only care about the 'benefits,' and this brings out the emotion which is the important side for your potential client to come on board.

What are the real benefits that you provide for your clients?

You can easily go about this by listing the features of what you do, and following it up with the benefits that it brings about.

For example.

> Feature is; providing high-quality fat and body composition testing
> The benefit is; to accurately track your progress and make tailored adjustments to your plan for faster results.
>
> Feature is; writing periodized workout programs that are synergistic with your nutrition plan.
>
> The benefit is; constantly upgrading your plan to achieve the most powerful results in the shortest time by avoiding plateaus and using advanced techniques such as 'nutrient timing' to excel your fat loss.

#4 - Define your promise

You do have to put your money where your mouth is and make a promise.

If you're too timid to take any real leap and make a promise, then you're not the highly-skilled professional you should be. This pledge to your clients will highlight the major benefit and differentiating factor that you bring to the world.

#5 - Combine it all

Now you take all the information that you have created from the above 4 steps and rework it into a paragraph that can simply roll off the tongue and be simply understood. Often there are recurring themes from what you have put together, so you want to merge these together.

#6 - Shorten it down

Now, edit it again, and make it shorter. How could this be put into 1 or 2 sentences that encapsulate everything.

This comes from the idea of having an 'elevator pitch' which is simply if you have 20 seconds to tell someone what you do then this is the phrase you say. The power behind this is that you want to clearly get across what you, the benefits, and the uniqueness that you bring are so they are pulling out their wallet or at least asking for more.

Once you've developed a USP, your job is to communicate it clearly and often, and it should weave in all your marketing and messaging.

Don't be scared that you're stuck with this forever, because I promise you that will not happen. Your USP is going to develop and change so be very willing to accept change and come back to this section to re-do the 6 steps.

I know myself that this has changed over 10 times in the last 5 years. As I've developed new businesses, created new passions, and learnt new skills I've wanted to take myself in new directions, work with different people, and create new levels of success.

I know, that this isn't going be easy, it's not meant to be, and one factor that will have you standing head and shoulders above your competition is that by doing this, they are not. Though don't think you will get it right straight away, continue to refine and get it crystal clear.

Go out and tell people, get feedback from the people that matter and you will then be able to use this USP through everything else moving forward in your business.

Now that you have created your USP, there is one major point that you cannot leave this chapter without mastering, and that is knowing your marketing inside and out. You need to know your potential client, what their goals and aspirations are, their fears and worries, what keeps them up late at night, and what their perfect dream would look like. You need to know your market so well you should be able to finish their sentences and then you will deliver what's needed.

Once you know your market intimately, you can then use everything I have going forward for you with so much more power. It changes the language you use, the messages you send to them, it ultimate changes how you deliver your services and results so you can craft the perfect way to deliver what they want, how they want.

This separates you and puts you ahead of your competitors by miles, and is also a major factor in how to have clients coming to you.

7 THE ESSENCE OF YOUR BUSINESS

To build your business, I have already shown that there are 3 basic principles of how this can be done.

1. Get clients to pay more per session/unit, for example, charging more per hour.
2. Get clients to pay you more frequently, for example, have more frequent sessions with you.
3. Offer clients other avenues of value with a greater range of products or services, for example, selling supplements.

We will be going through all three of these methods, but it's now important for you to grow a deeper understanding of what your business really is, and to change your outlook on how you are going to build and grow your success.

Most in your position right now and even you right now, think about the technical side of what you do. If you're a personal trainer, you think about the skills of program design, diet manipulation, and so as to best help get the client results. You wear the technician hat all day every day and love to read and learn about it. Though learning the latest bicep curl isn't going guarantee success, and even picking up and reading this book took a leap from your side that I appreciate. The other hat you must wear is 'sales' and I know I just scared you by saying the 'S' word, but hang with me.

If you truly are good at what you do, you get results for your clients, and you want to help people achieve great things and improve their lives, you NEED to be good at sales because I have seen this more times I care to count. Business owners scared of sales and because of that not willing to try, and then never be able to help people achieve results because they have no clients.

It is your duty to run your business like a pro – and one reason why I called my business mentoring business, Turning Pro Academy.

Now we can look at what the two basic areas of focus that boil down to creating a business that grows into the success you want.

Traffic and Conversions.

Traffic is about getting the right people that are your target market, the perfect type of client that you want to bring on board, and maximising how many of these people you can get. You want to build a know, like, and trust factor with every potential client. And you want to take them through the three steps of – not knowing who you are, to knowing who you are, engaging with you, to becoming a loyal client.

The last step entails conversions. This is turning a potential into a client. The truth is the traffic side, especially now, is very simple and a major focus of this book will be to show you how to simply set up traffic generating streams for your business running all day, every day and can be internationally focussed. Increasing traffic can be one of the easiest outcomes when using the easy to use online tools and content strategy I show you here. Being able to leverage things such as Facebook ads means you can hyper-target people worldwide, or just in your town and know the numbers of if it's working or not. I will not be delving into those more advanced tactics here in this book, as I want to give you the solid foundation that everything can be successfully built upon, and get you ready to use those strategies and tactics.

The real problem that you can have is an offer problem. Not having an offer that people are willing to climb through a snowy blizzard to get to. Then the next issue is being able to measure the effect of the traffic sources to that offer. Now, I'm not going to geek out on this, and I will give it to you in plain English.

As a great example of this is a client Michelle that came to me wanting to coach other bikini models as this is what she had a vast experience in. Being a competitor herself, she knew the ins and outs of how to get someone in amazing shape, though there was one big problem. All the programs she was trying to sell and her online personal training service were getting very little traction. After going through what she was initially selling, and her messaging behind what it was she was selling, it was really obvious what the problem was. She was being too broad with who she was trying to help. Michelle was clearly trying to attract not only other physique competitors but also the general population as well, which is a big killer to both sides.

As there is a big difference between what someone wants when they want to step on a stage in peak condition, compared to losing 10 pounds to feel good day-to-day. As this also goes into the psychology of what these different markets will need to achieve what they want, the system with which you use to deliver the results will be completely different.

After changing her basic message of what her offer was, she had a flood of new physique and bikini clients coming her way. That market finally saw in a clear and simple way that Michelle was offering what they wanted and would happily come on board.

Now it's time to:

- Increase the number of your clients
- Increase the average transaction per client
- Increase the number of transaction per customer

And by doing so, these three steps roll-up into a term called Customer Value Optimization.

So moving forward, there will be some steps you need to apply;

1. Have the perfect fit for customer and their problems with your solution, i.e. a product/market fit.
2. Choose a traffic source. Notice I didn't say 'sources,' I want you to start with one major traffic source first, become an ace in it, and then you can move onto another.
3. Offer value to them in exchange for their contact details or to engage with your business. This is where you can then continue to give more value, and also show them that you are the perfect solution (that's if you really are).
4. Educate and motivate them to come on board with a simple and very effective set of steps to convert them into the right solution.
5. Continue to grow and nurture the relationship, offer other

high-value solutions with products and services and build a lifelong relationship.

In the advanced coaching, such as the Pro Circle mastermind, we cover other steps either side and in more detail, though I know if you take these 5 steps and apply them to your business, you will have an engine that is powering and running continually to grow profits, success, and your lifestyle.

Now, you know how to look upon your business, what really matters when it comes to growing it, and it's now time to deep dive into the key strategies that will give you what you came here for.

PART 2
MARKETING

HOW TO ATTRACT CLIENTS

What happens to things you chase? ....they run.

Exactly like you trying to chase down clients, they run away and into the arms of your competitors. The focus that I am going to bring to you is how you can attract clients and have them coming to you. How you can engineer and set-up the steps so that you have them finding out who you are, discovering that you are the perfect solution for them, and then practically walking in the door ready to drop their credit card.

We want to develop the know, like, and trust factor that I mentioned before, this simply means that you're 'cool,' and you're not being a sleaze bag trying to be sneaky and 'hard sell' at all costs. Also by setting this up, and following this part of the book, this becomes an integral part of the engine that's running 24/7 for your business.

Being able to have people attracted to you and what you're offering, and them reaching out to want to learn more, or ready to come on board as your client for a premium is simply a set of actions that we set-up to happen.

The reason why in the first part we discussed and set up your USP is because this is going to flow through every part of your marketing. They language you use, the actual message and media in which you deliver it, and importantly who you deliver it to are all questions that need to be answered for marketing to become this client generating machine.

A fresh flow of new clients is the lifeblood of your business, and I will also be showing you how to maximise every client's lifelong value to your business, you will always need to be bringing in more clients.

1 – Identify your ideal client
2 – Discover where they hang out
3 – Know your business inside and out
4 – Position yourself as the answer
5- Use direct response to get results
6 – Build partnerships and JVs

There are multiple terms that come under marketing that will further highlight what we really do. Things such as permission marketing which is an approach to selling products or services in where a prospect agrees in advance to receive marketing information. An example of this is when you opt-in to my fitness and health site www. mybodyblends.com and opt-in for a free kick-start fat-loss diet, and I will follow-up and continue to give you exclusive access to videos, articles, and podcasts that will be perfect for you to get the results you initially signed up for.

Then there is inbound marketing in which you are attracting people to you, they are coming because you are giving value and they know you can help them solve the problem they have. Which then perfectly

Segway's over to content marketing, which will be the major focus on what you need to be doing.

This is NOT about setting up a blog, and just trying to fire out some articles and being ad-hoc about it, this is about you taking the stance and view that you are a publishing company as well. You need to be producing high-quality content that delivers bucket loads of value.

To have you standing head and shoulders above your competition and growing a fellowship of raving fans, I will show you how to have the content marketing side set up, but also importantly, how you can turn your following into customers and clients.

I also want to make the point that we are looking for more high-end clients, this is not about trying to get the bottom of the barrel or playing the price war and trying to be the cheapest. Cutting your price down as the only real avenue to entice and lure in clients is a fast-track to the bottom for you.

There are some major points that I will outline here, and these are baked into the rest of the book.

Let your price reflect the quality. 'Budget friendly' options or cutting your price lower than your competitor's is not a smart way to grow long-term success. Your profits are capped, and your potential to deliver greater value is cut off at the knee, whereas I would always rather add additional value and ensure greater results for my clients. High-end clients do not care much for the cheap provision, they do not trust them. Because everyone has been stung by trying to buy a cheap option and never getting the end outcome wanted.

This brings up the difference between cost and price. The price of something can be very cheap, but if it doesn't get you the result you want then you have to keep on buying, which means the total cost is much higher.

For example, if you choose a cheap plumber to come by and re-do your bathroom and two months later the pipes break, and you have to tear down the bathroom, including the tiling, to fix the plumbing, and your end-cost has gone sky high.

Your brand should reflect top quality, and the small attention to detail that can take you above and beyond your competitors is what will grow your name to be the best in the industry. This includes special bonuses for being a client of yours and over the top customer service.

One of the battles you must conquer is that these days we are all so immune to marketing messages, there is also the factor of how many times potential customers on average has to see your message to make a buying decision. This simply means that they need to see what you and your business is about, and be reminded of it multiple times before they are really say yes or no to your offer.

The route that a client takes to come on board is not seeing a Facebook post for the first time, clicking through, liking your sales page, and then pressing the buy now button to input their credit card and purchase. Coaching services don't get sold like that, there are certain steps that we take in making a buying decision, and once we engineer those steps in place and make it a part of your marketing engine then clients are pouring in by the boat load.

"Omnipresence' is a fancy word for being in multiple places. And this is where you want to take your marketing. You don't have to be everywhere, you just need to be in the main places your target market is hanging out. After using your research phase to know your client inside and out, you know where to put your marketing to have the best traction.

Other decisions would be what social media platforms would you want to focus on, what offline tactics would be key, such as magazines, publications, local meet ups, the options are endless, and you will cover this to be able to make the right decisions using the success sheets I have for you.

Ultimately you want need to create the right message that showcases what you do and have is the solution for the person's problem. You need to showcase that your solution is easy and effective along with having the unique qualities that give them what they want.

You then need to get in front of your market and showcase this, and I will be showing you in the next chapters how you showcase and build yourself as an authority to gain and then prove that you do have the right solutions. By giving them an actual solution, providing real value to them, you can start building the relationship, going through the steps of continually adding value, and answering key objections, which then leads to you offering your services and offers to take them on board as a client.

Now, the language I just used is so that this works for both face-to–face, online business, and all coaches and consultants.

Let me give you two real life examples of clients that I have done this with.

An offline example of this would be a dentist called Rob.

Rob specializes with kids, so has placed key, small, and powerful advertisements in school's publications, and with being able to reach the parents easily to showcase he gives free dental check-ups for kids. The parent rings up to book the consultation and the receptionist also takes down their email along with other information.

They email out 3 key emails from that day that showcase what the child will have done in the consultation, the results they get with testimonials, before and after shots, and answering key objections about getting further work done such as braces or invisalign. By the time the parents and child walks in for the consultation they already have an in-depth knowledge of what's going to happen, have been given great value to help them no matter what, and at the end of the consultation they are given a thorough report on what needs to happen for great dental health and aesthetics for the teeth of the child. The parent is brought in at the end of the check-up to go through this and then have them sign-up.

As a kicker for this process, every new client is asked, 'as a rule for coming on board with us, we ask that you refer two of your friends or colleagues to use us' and this referrals system is followed-up through mail, email, and in the next check-up.

This is a system that is generating numerous new clients on a weekly basis and filling up multiple dentistry's.

An online example would be an online personal trainer called Sophie.

Sophie wanted to start her online personal training business so she could give up her face-to-face work, earn more money, and to have freedom but struggled to know where to start. Once I coached her through what needed to happen, she now drives daily traffic to her site through articles and videos that she delivers multiple times a week.

She advertises her free value-packed content through Facebook, which means she is paying for people to see and read her free content. She now knows her market so well that her articles and videos are talking exactly about what they want to hear. Which for her she specializes in female stubborn fat loss for middle-aged women.

Talking about the hormonal environment, how the metabolism changes with age and other factors, and how to diet and train, her market joins up for her special offers which include ebooks that go deeply to give great answers and results, those ebooks then drive them to a webinar that she holds weekly.

This webinar again gives answers on exactly what these women want to know, and then shows them the next best step is to come on board her coaching packages. This is how she brings on new clients each week, and for a premium that is double the usual online trainer.

You can see in both of these examples with Rob and Sophie is there is a system in place that is scalable and repeatable. It grows to take in more people, and when we find something works like gangbusters, we feed it more.

This is what you are going to have by the end of this book.

8 BECOMING THE EXPERT

You need to become the 'go–to person,' the number one solution, the authority, the expert and the mini-celebrity in your niche. Earning your potential clients attention and then building a relationship with them which also showcases you as you as the authority. Will flip you from having to chase clients, to clients hunting you down.

There is the know, like, and trust factor that many marketers talked about and that I've mentioned before. I want to highlight this because it can be a simple understanding for how you need to go about attracting all the clients you want. Firstly, you need to get people that don't know you to know you – now this may seem beamingly obvious but what so many miss is that when reaching out to 'cold traffic' that is people that don't know who you are, then you need to jump some hurdles in which to make them go to 'warm traffic.' You need to give them bucket loads of value and talk to them and for them. Most people make a song and dance about how great their business is and all their credentials, but the prospect doesn't give a hoot about that.

They only care about themselves, (which we all do) and you need to feed that by talking to them about how they can solve the issue that they have. Then to create a like and trust factor, it firstly must come about that they must like you. First up, this happens by not using any 'douche-bag' tactics to get people attention or try to sell to them, and simply just be cool. Being a begging and wanting pleader for someone's business is never 'cool' and people will just walk on by.

The trust factor comes about when you need to deliver results, and by giving your value out, and them creating results even before they become a client is where you will create droves of people coming your way. Content, inbound authority marketing, whatever you want to call it, I'm just going to call it marketing for simplicity's sake moving forward. Though I will make the distinction that this is not traditional 'institutional marketing' where brand awareness is the goal. You don't have the budget or time to worry about brand awareness, what you need is to use direct response techniques to have the right people take an interest so you can hold their hand down the path to becoming your client.

Your website, in which I will go into detail soon, needs to become the hub for your business. Whether your business is 100% online, face-to–face, or a mix of both, this is where you can drive people to build those relationships. Now this isn't an internet marketing book, there are numerous offline internet marketing tactics that work wonderfully well for coaches, though I am going to focus on you having the right strategy in place to make the entire engine of your business work.

Most coaches that do tackle the content marketing simply have the plan that a 'to do' list of content to produce will suffice, this is not a strategy. These are the people that will get more eyeballs and traffic, though scratch their head when no more clients are coming on board. The entire process needs to be mapped out in that you want the people to follow through.

Firstly, you can understand that the entire process that you want people to go through looks like this:

1. Strangers – They don't know who you are, and this is referred to as cold traffic if you are sending our marketing messages to them. You want to be sending out high-value content to this group. In this phase, you are attracting people to you.
2. Visitors – This is when someone does come by your 'stuff' and checks you out. Your aim is to use a call to action (CTA) to collect their information, which could simply be name and email for you to further deliver great value to them. This phase is about converting people to become a lead.
3. Leads - So they have 'opted-in' and are wanting to know more about how you can help them. This is where you can use the power of email marketing to deliver great value, and then lead them through to a buying decision. This is the phase where you convert and close a client.
4. Clients – You've just landed a new client, but the fun doesn't stop here. This is where you need to maximise the experience, and you will also find that increasing the lifetime customer value is where true profits are found and exploded. This is where you deliver and delight.
5. Promoters – This is where you have delivered a world-class experience, they have great results and are now spreading the word for you and bringing in new leads and clients for you. You build upon and extend the relationship by also having increased options for how to serve them. This could be through an increased line to sell them, products, or services.

The process goes from attracting > converting > closing > delivering > nurturing. With each step having a specific purpose for how to move the right person through to the next step. Now this comes together and turns into the engine of your business when each of the 5 steps are in place and working, I understand it's pretty daunting looking at the above and knowing your current business is not set up like that at all, or there are holes everywhere.

Now, when I am coaching a business client, I dissect their business intensively to uncover all the bottles–necks and then work from the biggest one down so that results come thick and fast, and also so that we can uncover if there are more issues to be fixed. Though always working toward the end is that the business is humming along, with traffic coming in, clients being converted, world class delivery systems in place, and profits maximised.

We will focus on the first 3 steps now, later chapters will show you in detail in step 4 how to close and convert prospects to clients without being 'salesy'. Then having a referral system in place that uncovers one of the secret gems most coaches never uncover the full power of.

There is the rule of 'constant change.' And something you need to embrace as I am about to walk you through how you become the hot and well-known thing in your market and how you stay at the top.

Engineering how you get prestigious recognition is easy when you understand how it happens and the simple actions you need to take to make it happen. Being able to tap into the world of publications, columnist, radio shows with hosts, and TV shows with reporters that all need to be amazed by you and put their trust in you for you to deliver what their audience wants.

I first started out by getting written articles into a fitness magazine. A few months of constantly getting my work published in them and I was able to grow a relationship with the editor, and she appreciated the effort of me coming forth with great articles and new ideas. I was then able to snag the job of shooting workout articles and images for the magazine, which even lead to a few video commercials.

From there I was able to go to other publications that were bigger, and get published always being able to reach up to a bigger and better opportunity as each time they saw the work I produced and had the praise of the last people I worked with.

This is the same now that I run two podcasts, the My Body Blends podcasts are dedicated toward getting people in great shape, and Ask The Pro podcasts are dedicated toward fitness business success. One of the biggest reasons I love spending the hours in publishing episodes each week is that I am able to interview and chat with world class guests. I'm able to get them onto my shows for free and spend time growing a relationship with them.

The aim is that I'm always in it to help them as much as possible, I'm there to help grow their audience and promote their business. The massive win for my audience that tunes in each week is that they get world best insights and value from every episode. Then this is able to lead onto not only just having a great network of quality people, but it also leads on to partnerships, joint ventures, and them growing my business and brand as well.

Another evolution you need to stay on top of is creating new products and services. Being able to stay with the trends and up to date with trade magazines, news, and industry or niche specific publications both online and offline will have you tuned into what the market is looking for.

This is where using the top fitness magazines as a resource to know what topics they are publishing, and the language and words they are using to sell their magazines. Many fitness professionals snub their noses at the main stream magazines because they think the quality of the content isn't high, but you need to think deeper.

This is where understanding the market of the publication and how the magazine is speaking to them comes in. New product and services ideas will flow from this one tactic alone for research, and it will become a library for helping you develop sales copy to sell your offers.

Tieing into seasons and holidays is an easy way to develop your marketing calendar to have themes, and give you current events that you can promote and give value on. A great example of this is when Christmas and New Year comes around each year, how you can be helping people to not gain weight over the holidays, and how to make the right choices with their foods or get effective short workouts in if they are travelling.

Now, you need to focus on producing the content that is going to showcase the knowledge and skills you have, and then get it in front of the exact right people so this becomes a funnel that will literally end up with you having new clients and customers signing up each week. The first question you need tackle is what content are you going to produce, as you have the options of writing, visual, and auditory. The key here is to start with only one, and this is the one that you feel is your strength. If you're a great writer, then write great articles, or if you can get in front of the camera, then produce videos. Now, if you were to look at myself and many others as an example, you will see that I do all three types of content, though I didn't start out that way. It's step-by-step, for when I started shooting videos, that is all I did as there is a learning curve, and the more you practice and produce, the better you get. Only recently I had to go through my video library and delete quite a few of the old ones and make notes for me to re-shoot those topics again. It was horrible to watch, and I laughed at myself at how bad it was. With practice, I've got no problems with getting in front of the camera and talking in-depth on topics.

With the podcasts, the skill of interviewing, and being able to deep-dive into one topic has been something I have loved learning. And when really getting into building two podcasts, which at the point of writing a third podcast is about to be started. With over 150 podcast episodes under my belt, and numerous episodes where I have been interviewed, I now feel comfortable in doing it, but always knowing there is still so much to learn. As the goal isn't to be perfect at them, it's to produce value for the listener, viewer, or reader.

The next part of the content marketing equation you need to piece together is now the, "what topics do I produce content on?"

This is where research is going to do you a world of good, and just like researching the market when you were finding out about your target-market and who your competitors were, it's time to go back and look at what people are engaging with. Go to your top competitors and see what topics they are producing content on. An easy way to do this and to also find what people are engaging with is to go to your competitors YouTube channels, go to their video page and select 'view most viewed option.' This will show you in descending order their top viewed videos, and give you a great snapshot of what people

are watching. What are the top searched for terms in Google, by going to the Google keyword planner tool, this will show you what people are typing into Google and searching for.
Then you need to have a system in which you can manage everything as I see two major segments of both my businesses being 'publishing.' They are just like a magazine, or TV shows would treat the content that they produce, I want the exact same focus on this, and this can be done by putting together an editorial calendar.

As a bonus, I will include a template editorial calendar in the downloads for you as this will show you what quick info you need to track to make sure you are producing, publishing, and sharing out your content. As I know it all too well, when you're busy trying to build your business, work with clients, and living a life things get lost and forgotten about. So the editorial calendar I use and collaborate with 3 other team members is a key piece in making sure everything else runs smoothly.

How often you produce content is up to how dedicated you are, as you can produce one video every day if you set your sights on it. I know this can be daunting for you, but at the same time being realistic of what you can produce, I also know by sitting in the position as your coach that you need a good kick up the backside to push harder.

The other side of trying to go too hard and fast into this is the imbalance between being qualitative and quantitative. And that is producing too much content, but it's not of great quality or value. I would much rather see you produce 2 to 3 great pieces of content per week that really drive home great amounts of value for your target market. Then the aim is to build upon this as you get better because I also know when you first start out at this, it's foreign, its hard, and its takes a lot of time. So as you become more effective and efficient in producing content, and able to take on at least one team member that could be a virtual assistant, you are then able to give time-consuming tasks away and focus on what is most powerful for your business growth.

9 NEW GENERATION MARKETING

There are two key concepts that you have to understand that so many are still lagging on. These problems are causing a major disconnect from how people are trying to attract and sign on clients, to growing a following, to increasing profits.

We've all seen it before, and yes, I will even touch on how you can do it properly as a strategy that plugs into the business so effectively. The ebooks, guides, diets, online newsletters, etc. that are all asking you to sign up to get access to something. Now, this is a needed tactic to use in your online business, as you want to grow your email list. But before we jump into how you do it, there is a fundamental way you need to do this differently from others. Everyone is trying to get you to sign up to their email lists, and stepping into the shoes of your potential customers that are bombarded with diets, workouts, supplements that your competitors trying to latch on to and turn them into a customer.

These days it's not about getting the sign-up and then trying to build the relationship, which is actually a step forward to what so many people do and still do to this day, it is just going straight for the sale. A common scenario that you can see today is the Instagram personalities trying to sell their programs or service straight from their bio or the one link they get in their profile.

With everyone's guard constantly up, trying to protect themselves from all the different offers and marketing messages, there is one clear winning way to step above your competitors. And that is to build relationships through giving value first. And doing so over and over again. As the general tactic online marketers would use before would be to focus on getting a person to opt-in first, and then build a rapport and relationship in a short time to then move onto fast-tracking the sale.

This problem with that is now people are suspicious of opting in for free guides, or what we call lead magnets, which are pieces of value in which you give away for someone email. The beauty about this problem is that it's easy to not have a problem with opt-in if you are focussing giving great value, and then once you know that is done, only giving those people the offer for them to opt-in and take the next steps moving forward.

Especially with the power that Google and Facebook give you with online marketing, you can put ads right in front of the people that you know that have either visited certain pages on your website, or have watched a video for a certain length of time, and a mind blowing other amount of ways you can segment a huge market. This is about making sure that you are only talking to the right people, and following up with those people as you know they are highly interested and engaged with you and what you do, and you can give them an offer that matches what their issue is.

A great example of this is with email marketing automation. Let's say we have a campaign that starts out as a fat-loss diet plan. In certain emails, we can have links that are specially made for males to click on and others for females to click on. So already we have segmented them into male and female. We can take it further with this example, and say with the females we have links for burning stubborn fat, other for cellulite and others for fast weight-loss for a special event. Now we segmented the females into three categories, and each time that they click on a link, they automatically get moved onto a specific sequence of emails that is only talking about that direct issue and interest they have, which further means you are giving them the value that is highly relative to them, plus you can make an offer of a program, service, or product that you know is very much what they are looking for.

Another example is that we can use tracking with the email and websites so that if someone is hitting certain articles or videos of yours over and over, and they start performing other actions such as filling out a questionnaire, or replying to emails, and so on, they can have a score added to them. Say each time they watch a video it's worth 2 points, if they open your email, it's worth 1 point if they reply to your email it's worth 3 points, and on it goes. You can have a tipping point for if someone hits a total score of 30 points, it alerts you, and it can even start a new sequence just for that person. If someone is constantly engaging with you and your content, then you know they are highly interested, and they are the best person for you to reach out to and convert into your customer or client.

The second biggest issue is having the wrong focus on social media, as all too often I see people get swept up with the 'vanity metrics' of likes and followers. I know plenty of personalities in the fitness world that have a huge number of social media followers, but it doesn't equal monetization. So this is when you need to look at social media like a satellite, and its aim is to bring them back to your main hub.

This is why in the next chapter I will walk you through why your main hub is your own website, and how you should really focus on building your own platform and assets. By saying this, I don't want you to not use social media, or think that I'm poo-pooing its importance. It's very important, and can be hugely powerful when used right, and if you're feeling right now that you've tried social media to grow your business, and you haven't got the traction, growth, or clients from it, then don't worry. I will walk you through what needs to happen to make sure you grow your following and turn them into your customers and clients.

Just as I was talking about before with you needing to give value first and have people attracted to you and what you are offering, social media is where you need to choose the right platform and use it as a way to syndicate your content out but always making it native to the platform.

For instance, you can write a great article and put it on your website. Though you will want to share this to get as many viewers as possible, you need to share it through whatever social media platform you use. Though they are all different, and need to be treated differently. What you do on Instagram won't work on what you do on Facebook, or Snapchat, etc. So the first decision you need to make is what platform will you focus on, and only choose one. Get really good at one platform before you move onto others, as it's spreading yourself too thinly that can kill your efforts to really making it work. Making sure the platform you choose is 1) where your target market is, and 2) you enjoy working with.

When you have your website as your hub, your social media platforms as your satellites bringing people back to your hub, and your email as another powerful touch point, you will see when I touch on the power of omnipresence later in this chapter that this is the perfect storm for building your online business.

Generating droves of new clients coming into your inbox, begging to come on board, or knocking on your front door ready to start with you is an ideal situation when we tick just a few simple boxes that are coming up. Until now I have focussed on how you can become a better entrepreneur and business owner, how to truly take charge of your business, and the have the overview of attracting in new clients.

The fact is, your market has more options than they can poke a stick at when it comes to choosing a coach, or even another means of solving their issue. For example, let's take an online personal trainer – the battle you have on your hands is separating yourself from all the other online trainers around the world, you also need to differentiate yourself from online membership sites that can deliver meal plans, training programs, and more. Then you also have to deal with if the potential client wants to hire a face-to-face personal trainer.

Firstly, there are the qualifications that you want to use such as, online personal training isn't a great choice for a brand new beginner to training. They need the physical hand-holding, guidance, and teaching in how to train properly first, so online coaching works much better for more experienced trainers. Having those disqualifications work for you and tying that into your target market that we have covered, you still have to compete with your competitors.

We showcased how having a strong and clear 'uniqueness' of a marketing message is the first step to making this happen, it's not the time for you to broadcast this to the world and be known what you want to be known for. This is where the power of content marketing comes in, and also using the position of authority and the next chapter of having a platform to showcase this for yourself and your business.

Content marketing is the focus in producing a high-quality value that is creating, publishing, and distributing for your target audience, usually online and with the goal of attracting, converting, and retaining clients. Now most people just use content to attract clients, though I see it as very powerful to help with the conversion process, and also in delivering results and retaining clients. The most common components of a content marketing plan would be through social media platforms,, your own platform (very important, and the next chapter), and include content assets, such as articles, podcasts, videos, ebooks, and webinars.

An example of how this works is that you start producing hyper targeted articles to solve the problems and give advice for your target market, and then syndicate this through all your social media platforms, email lists, and networks. As people are finding out that they need to get in shape and do something about their weight, they start searching for answers, and your content is coming up, and they realise you offer the coaching and services for weight loss. They will continue to soak up the information, and this is where you want to then use the content to drive them to the next step of converting them to your email list or how you want to continue to build that relationship. You have created the know-like-trust factor by giving great advice and value through content they wanted to consume, and you are the number one choice they go to when it's time to choose a trainer or coach.

The buying cycle for someone wanting to hire a coach isn't a split decision, this isn't like buying a Coke on your walk home. People nowadays are bombarded with marketing messages all day every day, and it's the fact of being everywhere all the time, to be omnipresent, to have enough interactions with them that will lead to them taking the next steps.

Think about how you can be everywhere for them. They came across a short training video and status on Instagram and followed your page because it gave great tips. Then later that day they went onto Facebook and there you are again, another blog article of yours comes up. Then not long after, a video of you comes up in Facebook, and it's a quick spiel on how you are giving away a free training program. They think, "Oh wow, that's exactly what I need, and it's free." The fact is though, when they read your blog article you used a re-targeting pixel to have a low-cost ad pop-up with that video that's targeted to convert prospects to leads. They then get your emails after signing up and keep seeing more posts come up on their social media feeds.

You will be shown later how simple internet marketing tactics can be easily used to have this new generation of marketing become a system that is creating new clients by the day. Because the real power of this is that it's scalable, you are able to talk to the masses but be so specific who you get your marketing message to.

10 YOUR EXPERT PLATFORM

You need to become an authority, which simply means you're not only a thought leader on a specific topic, you have also taken the time and effort to translate that knowledge in a meaningful way and delivered it. And by being the business owner, you have this content spread through the net effectively to reach the eyeballs you want, your prospects and customers recognize it and as a result, it helps you generate a constant flow of new customers and profits.

It's no secret now, people do business with other people they trust, and by putting yourself out there and giving your brand a personality, and taking the time to present great quality value that actually helps others solve problems in the area you are the 'authority' you develop trust on a large scale.

It's now time to build your platform in which your business will grow, and with the current trend of growing social media followings, the ego gets a kick when your Facebook, Instagram, or any other social media followings go up – but is it actually growing your profits?

This is an important question as being in the health and fitness world, there are plenty of people that have huge followings and likes, but it doesn't translate over to be monetizable unless done properly. The true number that would be better to look at when translating over to profits is your email list. This is not poo-pooing social media at all, I see it as an integral part for much of business, though there is a step so many fail to follow through with that crushes their business growth. And the basis here is that you want to be taking people off social media and bringing them to your own platform, and that is your website, and also converting them onto your email list.

Coming soon I will be outlining some marketing tactics including internet marketing tactics that are about list and audience building and how to convert those into customers and clients. Now, you only need to work on building your platform, driving people to it, and having the simple steps in place to start the conversion process and building profits.

I get a lot of personal trainers coming to me wanting to come on board the coaching programs, and a part of the interview process before starting is seeing what online presence they have and looking at if they have a website, what's missing or broken to make powerful changes to it. Too much of the time the websites look great, it's a fancy looking brochure, talking about themselves and what credentials that have, but it's not making them any more money. It's collecting cyber dust and wasting time and money.

You have to ask yourself three questions with your current website (if you don't have one now, its ok, you will use this section to get a working and profit producing site up).

1. Is it building my profits?
2. Is it driving traffic for me?
3. Is it converting people to what I want?

Most of the time the answer to number 1 is no. And that's OK because you probably don't even know how it correlates over to your profits, it's not just about having people buy from your site, as for coaching, this happens only a small amount of the time. Then you need to know whether the site is driving more people to itself. Are new people finding you, and are people coming back? Then you need to know if your site is actually getting people to go to the next step you want.

As I said, it's not always about having people click the 'buy now' button on your site, and you get money, as being a coach this doesn't happen a lot of the time. And why I ask the question in the way I did is because much of the time the purpose of your site is actually to convert people to list building.

Your email list as mentioned before is a powerful asset for your business, especially when used right. This is why having your site's main priority in driving people to build your list you are then able to build on those relationships, weed out the wrong people, and then offer the right people the right programs or services and have them come on board as a client.

So to boil it down for you, your website is an 'authority site,' and this is where its readers place their trust due to both the quality of its content and the quality of their experience. Then because both of these are great, the user is happy to take the next step and sign up for a 'lead magnet' and engage further with you and even share content out for you.

Once you've helped the readers once, and if the experience was seamless, a good proportion will start reading more of your site, and the relationship builds. This is about building long-term relationships versus a one night stand. Most people think it's about getting someone to land on their site and then buy straight away, this just does not often happen anymore, and especially for you being a coach.

For you to create your authority site, you need to truly help the readers and offer expert advice. You also need to be the recognizable person behind it and give it a personality. And finally, you need to focus on building engagement on the site.

Let's face the facts now, building the authority site is going to take longer, it's going to take a lot of your time, especially at the start when you can't outsource a lot and the energy cost will be big because you have to produce high-quality, high-value content. You are the expert, and I know because you are reading this that technically you are good at what you do, you get results for your clients, you just now need more clients and to have the business working for you to take that leap to success.

Now I know I've dropped some words that you might want to know more about, and this ties everything together for you to use this. I said you would offer a 'lead magnet' from your website, this is simply a piece of high-value information you give in exchange for their contact details such as email and name. We have all seen the 'sign up for my newsletter' links, though these days, it's more likely eBooks to sign up for. But to be truly standing head and shoulders above your competition, you need to deliver great value that's quick and easy to consume and actually gets them results. It can be a short cheat sheet, a checklist, a resource guide, a video guide, a webinar, or a presentation; there are numerous options you can have. You choose whatever best suits your market, how they want to consume information, and how it's going to work best for them.

Also, the type of value you give on your site can vary, I referred to your website visitors as 'readers' though you don't have to produce articles. The media you choose is up to you, you can only do videos, or audio in the form of podcasts, again the options are numerous, though my advice is to choose only one form initially. Get really good at it and then you can branch out to others.

Myself at the moment, I produce articles, videos, and podcasts for both my fitness and business sites, there is a lot of content going out. To be upfront though, I have a team that takes on the great workload of making that happen. They help create, produce, publish, and syndicate the content, so my job now is to only deliver the expert advice.

The other important part of your site and content is that you need to talk in the language of your audience. All the time in the fitness world, I see trainers and coaches produce mediocre content, and it's worded with language that is trying to impress their colleagues, not their audience. If your marketing is middle aged women that are trying to lose a few kilos and feel confident, then don't be talking jargon and scientific terms trying to sound smart. It's going to go right over their heads, they won't be able to use it, and will move onto the next person that gives them what they actually want and need.

Publishing high-value content, targeted towards answering the key questions and solving the problems that your market is having, is going to build you as a credible source. Your website is to become a hub of information where people come back to again and again. This is also a perfect opportunity to use case studies of the results with your clients, as this works in two very powerful ways. One, you will be delivering answers and inside information for how your clients have achieved results that show the audience what they need to be doing in a similar situation. And two, by showcasing these results, you are showcasing yourself as the expert, as you are the catalyst and expert that is making the results come about.

11 DEVELOP A MARKETING STRATEGY

This is not going to be like the infamous 'business plan' that is said that everyone should toil over before starting their business. This is an actionable set of steps you are going to walk through, so that each day and week, you know what needs to be done, and you can easily follow through. This stems straight from having that clear description of who your target audience is. Though now, it's time for you to set your objectives and what are the goals you are striving for.

Just saying "I want more clients" is not going to do you any good. There is a need to be concise, such as "To convert 3 new clients per week into my $300 a week program." This then shows you that your growth should be an added $900 of recurring income a week, and importantly we can now set out how this is going to happen.

If you don't know the numbers of what's to come, have an estimate, and this will be an important side note; know your numbers and track what's happening. For this example let's say, it takes 3 sales conversation on average to convert one new client. And for every 3 sales conversations, it takes 10 email enquiries to come in.

From this alone, you know that you need 30 email enquiries coming in each week to grow your business by an added $900 each week. By using more advanced strategies, such a conversion rate optimization (which is just a fancy word for making each step better) is possible. You can improve each step by a small amount. This now means you convert one out of every two sales conversations, and you convert 10 email enquiries into 6 sales conversations. Which just by those increases in each step of the funnel you're now converting. So with just 30 email enquiries, the same number still coming in, you're now converting 9 new clients a week, which would be an added $2,700 a week.

Then let's say with this example that after improving those steps, you focused on your content marketing to drive more people to your site and then improved the number of email enquiries coming in through better email marketing on your behalf, you doubled it by having more precise email relationship building and better content that was more shareable that brought more people to your site initially. From that, it increases your email enquiries from 30 to 60 a week, and you're now converting 18 new clients with those same numbers as before, and each week growing your business by an added $5,400 each week.

Looking back at the steps, there is not a lot there, and especially by taking each step and improving it by a small amount and then moving on, the goal of bringing in an additional $900, has now turned into a real life growth of bringing in $5,400 each week. This is the type of growth that catapults your business to a bigger size than you thought possible and really sets you up with a business that gives you the money, freedom, and lifestyle you want. But, let's also be honest, the above is more than realistic, and I know it can happen.

But it cannot happen if you do not follow the steps I lay for you throughout this book.

You will not be able to achieve this because there will be bottlenecks, such as the actual capacity to serve all those added new clients to the business, or you cannot take on the number of enquiries coming in, or no way to handle how to convert them into the sales conversation. This is why, having a business that is selling time-for-money straight out like personal training will never lead to this type of income, business, or success.

So now it's time to lay out the marketing strategy so that you can have this type of growth in your business.

With the goals of your marketing are you wanting to:

- Increase brand awareness in key markets?
- Drive referral traffic back to your website?
- Increase sign ups and list building?
- Convert into new clients?

Also, notice that none of the above are about 'vanity metrics' such as likes, followers, or shares.

The checklist to follow is:

1. Understand your audience. I know this is the third time I've said this so far, it's that important. If you don't know your audience and market inside and out, it's time to spend more time researching and understanding.
2. Identify the right content formula. This is about connecting what you are comfortable with, what you are good at, and how

your audience wants to consume content. If your market is all about watching videos, then I would highly recommend you produce video content. Also, being comfortable is a two-edged sword. On one side, you have it working for because you can get started, on the other you need to challenge yourself and understand we all start somewhere. Knowing the right formula also means mapping out the structure and framework in which you will create your content. Such as what will the flow be for your videos. Having a framework to use is one of the best, more effective and easiest ways to get into producing high-quality content each time.

3. Create an editorial calendar. This is where you need to turn 'pro,' and not be ad-hoc about your content creation. Setting up an editorial calendar will outline when you will create, what topics, what the deadlines are, and other specificities you need to follow when it comes time to following through.
4. Syndication. This is getting the most mileage out of your content and 'snowballing' it to have a greater reach and more eyeballs. For example, I can turn the same content I used to record a podcast and shoot a video from it. Then I have someone transcribe that video and have it turned into an article. From the article, images, and social media statuses are produced. So one main piece of content turns into multiple which gives you more time and grows your reach. Syndication also takes into account where will you be sharing this content out, and how people will connect with it. Is it through your email list, other emails lists, or social media platforms? This is for you to decide.
5. Measure progress and update. You need to know what's working and whats not, simply pumping out content for 3 to 6 months and not getting a lot of traction can be demoralising to you. Knowing what topics, what content,

and what platforms are giving you the best results gives you a clear path on what to hone in and work on more.

As we touched upon in the first part of the book, it's now time to switch from outcome focused to behavioural focused. This is where the rubber meets the road, and you get moving on what needs to be done.

You need to outline and set when it is you are going to follow through and execute on each of the actions you need. I would recommend you only forecast 12 weeks ahead, and then re-plan from there by looking and reviewing what has worked and not worked. By giving yourself 12-week blocks to work in, you focus on what needs to be done without getting caught up in long term thinking. Which saves you from the constant changes we all experience that will throw out any long term plan.

You want fast results, and there isn't anything wrong with that, in the day of instant gratification, everyone is looking for the quick fix. Though I hope you're a step ahead, and can understand that you also need to plant seeds and give them time to grow. A common question that I get is "how quickly can I get to my goal?" – this could be to get to the amount of clients they want, or income they want, or any other metric they are focussed on. Which is no problem in doing so, as I also know that there is a certain level of pain from your current situation that you want to change. The pain of not loving the work you're currently doing, or not earning the money that you want and the stresses that come with all of that. So you want to get out of that pain, and start enjoying the job of truly running a business that has the positive impact you know you can create on the people.

Meet Brad, as this is an example of how you can use the 5-steps above along with everything else I've given you in this book so fast-track your own success. When Brad came to me, he had zero online assets, website, or social media following. He was a great coach and had the skills and know-how to really transform bodies and lives, though was fed up with working in a gym and paying rent knowing at the end of each day he wasn't having the security of a true business.

Brad quickly got the clarity as he already had a good idea that his target market was professional corporate males, and from working with this market for some time, he had the daily conversations of what their struggles and pains were. So it didn't take long, after some research, to outline what were the major topics that he needed to produce content on and share out. Also, using his current assets of his face to face personal training business and clients, he could have his clients share his content out through their networks, which then allowed him to quickly build his list and following by using Facebook alone.

The biggest issue Brad had when he came to me was that he didn't have a lot of free time, already having a full client book and family with the responsibilities that come with it. I wanted to make sure that everything he was doing to build his online fitness business was exactly as needed. This is also why you can use face-to-face coaching and the online business working together. Even if you want to continue doing your face-to-face personal training and have the online business on the side, this is easily done as you just have to link what you do for one, can be transferred over to the other.

Go through the 5 above points again with a crystal clear vision of what your objective and goal is. Then list out everything you must do, and break it down into the behaviours you must follow on a weekly and a daily basis, and what actions you need to be making that will lead to the outcome you want. This is setting out on what you need to follow through with.

For example, when writing this book for you, the behaviour I set myself from the very beginning was to write for a minimum of 45 minutes every morning as the first task I did. After going through my morning routine of getting my brain and body ready for the day, I started writing. I knew roughly how long I wanted to make this book, and could gauge how many words I was producing in each writing session. I quickly knew how long it would take me to get the first draft written.

On the other hand, I also publish a lot of videos for both the fitness and physique business along with my business mentoring. For this, I set the behaviour of having two video shooting sessions per week. This is where for at least an hour, I would get in front of the camera and deliver answers to the very questions I was getting asked from my audience. From this, I know how many episodes I can produce, and then map out when they would be getting published by using my editorial calendar.

PART 3
CONVERSIONS

12 THE CLIENT PIPELINE

Your client pipeline is going to become a funnel that will be mostly working on auto-pilot by generating and even converting them, so they come straight to you with payment already made.

Just like a water pipeline, a marketing pipeline can get clogged and need cleaning and maintenance. This is where we want to also overcome bottlenecks before they arise so that you are not capping your potential and success. We also want leads to be flowing into your pipeline from multiple channels, all capable of moving towards converting as your clients.

The pipeline should always be working, if you drop the ball and don't maintain the pipeline, the flow dries up, and it's hard to refill it again. You want to maintain the flow the whole time, and this is where it is so important to have multiple pieces automated, or other team members helping.

The filters we need to place throughout your pipeline mean by the time someone gets to the end of the funnel, they are qualified and are your perfect client. You don't want the wrong type of person coming on board, as we all know this can be a major drain on yourself and your business. There is also the time someone can spend in the pipeline before coming on board as a client, or falling off. Some people will need a considerable amount of time, and some can feel like they just flew straight in.

Filling your pipeline with quality leads is crucial, as you want to be able to have the end result as someone who; is able to economically buy, the right fit for your business and value, and has the right problem that you and your business can solve. This is where if you are trying to chase multiple rabbits – you won't catch any. So the case is true for being selective as to who you take on board, and what leads you to want to follow through with. Not everyone is the right fit for your business, and that's a good thing.

This is where I use and show my members the 4-step perfect client pipeline.

These are the simple 4-steps which you can set up to flow so that at the end from a lead coming in, you are able to have them come on board as a perfect client.

It's broken down into:

- The jaw-drop event: Where you are positioning yourself and the 'answer' by being a credible expert with the know-how and skills.
- Funnel Formula: This is where you can easily clear out time-wasters, and have the perfect fit move forward and fill up your sales appointments in a streamlined process.
- The Consultation: This is where you need to learn about them, their situation, and what it's going to take to solve their issue and deliver results.
- Strategy Session: This is where you walk them through

the solution, and make the go or no-go decision. Simply connecting the dots for them coming on board and having the solution they need.

I loved this whole process when I first learnt and started applying it, as it flipped the psychology and situation. No longer was I chasing after clients. Instead, they were coming to me, and I had my 'red velvet rope' in the way, making sure they were the right fit before coming on board. They were jumping through the hoops to show that they were able to start with me.

Let me walk you through these 4-steps so that you can start applying this from today. I also have a download that puts this into a step by step plan, and more insights for you to use by going to the downloadable work sheets.

1.

The jaw-drop event is really a host of different events, though there will always be one that 'broke the camel's back' and got them to take the next move. This is where your content marketing is so crucial, as each time someone consumes your content, it is an event. And you can build upon this by continually following up with them and being seen and in the top of their mind.

A great example of this is when they publish your content through your social media, let's say to be specific, Facebook. They come across your content one day on Facebook and click to read an article on your site. Now through the ease and wonder of re-marketing, by them landing on your website and you using a 'cookie' that tags them, you're now able to advertise more content of yours to them again not only on Facebook but also on other mediums such as Youtube and Google. This is where the omnipresence idea is so powerful. It's almost like you're stalking them through the internet. But it's just you giving them more chances to consume more great content from you, and this is where you use it as well to make them an offer.

You offer them even more value in exchange for their name and email, and this builds your email list. This is a true asset when used properly for your business, and because you can then move onto step two.

2.

Your funnel formula is simply a set of steps that takes someone from not knowing you, to know-liking-trusting you and to the third step. This funnel is commonly used with email marketing, where your goal is to deliver great value and build a relationship with them.

You have to give them a very good reason to spend the time to open, read, and use the emails you send through. And by talking about and helping them with the very problems they have and are related to why they joined in the first place, you are able to clear out the time wasters and then give them the right offers to fill up your sales appointments.

(Don't let the words "sales appointments'" scare you. These are simply just steps 3 and 4 of the process and are done in a non-douche-bag salesy way)

The offer could be a "free weight loss consultation," where you will assess what is needed so that you can come together with the plan needed for them to ultimately get the results they want. This process is set up so that even if they don't come on board as a client by their or your decision, they are still walking away with a positive experience, and help so they can get results.

3.

The consultation is where you get straight into finding out how you can develop the plan, and what that plan will be for them to get the results they have come to you for. This is where you need to ask many smart questions to unveil what it is that's holding them back, and what it's truly going to take.

You need to diagnose the problem with this step before giving the prescription. And when you think about what most coaches do when a lead comes to them, or even asks about their services or price. They jump straight into their packages, what they offer, and the next steps. This is a huge mistake, as this is prescription before diagnosis, and within the medical field, this is illegal.

You need to pin-point the problem first. This will position you as the expert, and you are able to lead them into the strategy session if they are the right fit.

4.

This is selling without selling.

The strategy session is where you give what the plan needs to be for them to achieve the results you both have talked about previously together. By walking them through the solution again, you are seen as the expert, you can also cover all objections that may stop someone from starting as a client by having this in place.

If they are the right fit, and they can see the solution that's needed for them, tailored to fit their needs, then you are able to show them the door to coming on board as a client.

These four steps will take the prospective clients through the needed questions to make sure of by the time someone is at step four; they are the right fit for your solution, you have a detailed plan as to how best to serve them, they are someone that you want to work with, and they are in the right position to make a decision whether to purchase or not.

All four steps are highly applicable to both your face-to-face business and online fitness business, as we can use the example of online personal training. Kathy, who came to me just wanting to have a high-end 1on1 online personal training service, knew she was good at what she did. She had a very high level of expertise, and for her to truly give her expertise to equal clients results, she wanted to work with a small number of clients at once, all one on one.

A big problem she was having was that she could only take on a select type of client, and obviously, her having a high level of service and charging what she was worth the cost of coming on board with Kathy, meant that this was 5-6 times more than the average online personal trainer. We were able to distil her marketing and sales strategy using the four steps outlined above by having a video over 30 minutes in length that people would opt-in for, whereby she thoroughly went through what the major problems, pains, and solutions were with her target market. From there, she had the offer for anyone who watched her video to come onto a free weight loss consultation with her so she could outline what that person's true issues are and what was needed to solve them.

The power of these first two steps is that she is able to very clearly show to the people what real problems they are having and talk to them in their language. Making it simple to understand, these potential clients knew that Kathy had a deep understanding of what they were going through. Then by having a second consultation, where Kathy would walk them through what steps they would need to take to get the results they said they wanted to achieve, it was a very natural progression that they would sign on with Kathy. This whole process was engineered to make sure that the people that were coming onto the first consultation were a great fit and highly motivated to get results. If she offered them the second consultation, it was because she knew that she could help, and just needed to time to map out what the solution needed to be. Then by the end of the second consultation, the prospect would have already built a great rapport with her, they know that she has a deep understanding of the problem at hand, and Kathy has given them the outline of what the solution is.

Now, granted, there is more to this process than just slapping a 'buy now' button on your website or social media post, but this is a process that means you are taking on the right clients and charging what you're worth, and I always am confident of my members that take on this process that it grows a long lasting business with security.

13 SELLING IS NOT A DIRTY WORD

Every business is broken down into two main actions, and yours is no different. It must deliver its service or produce its products, and this is where most business owners get caught up and tangled in spending all their time. They are trying to improve their product or service without ever knowing exactly what to fix, or if it needs to be fixed at all.

The other main action is the tie-in with marketing and sales. And with the common thread of 'sales' and being a 'salesman' as dirty words, it's a notion you need to stamp out from right now. The truth is you are selling every single day whether you like it not. You are selling yourself, your ideas, your business, your services, and more. When you want to go to a restaurant, you're selling your idea to your wife on why the steak house will be a great option. When you get a craving and want ice-cream, you're selling to yourself, and justifying why it's ok to go eat ice cream tonight.

I know that you are doing what you're doing because you want to help people, and you're good at what you do. You being a coach means you can have a powerful impact of your client's lives, they can live happier, with more confidence, healthier, and with longevity because of what you do. You think of yourself as a coach and not a salesman, and that's where I say you are wrong and that you are both.

You won't have the clients to be able to powerfully impact their lives if you don't sell yourself and your services. Those clients will go to someone else. They will happily pay your competitor, and you will miss out. I say happily pay because they will, people are not going to give up their hard earned cash for something they don't want.

The other problem that's stopping most coaches from reaching their own success, and this can very well be yours as well is the low self-esteem of not caring what you're worth. It's going to be very tough for you to close deals if asking for enough money is a problem for you.

This is where the first problem you need to overcome is, you standing in your own way. Use these 5 steps to stop being the barrier to further success and excelling your business growth.

1. Know your value to your clients: What does it cost to your client to have their problem solved? And then ask yourself; what are the benefits you are providing, including emotional benefits your clients have by going from where they are now to where they want to go?

This really shows that what you're doing impacts your clients and improves their lives in many ways. For me and my business mentoring clients, it's easier to see a monetary form of improvement. If a client comes to me and she is earning $75,000 a year and tirelessly working around the clock, and then she goes to earning $200,000 a year, and is working 5 half days a week and has freedom to work from anywhere, there are many benefits. The obvious benefit is the extra $125,000 she earns per year, the other improvements are what it is worth to her to have freedom to live and work in any location, and halving her time in her business.

For a personal trainer, the improvements can be the self-confidence that comes with a stronger, leaner body. They are happier, and their health means they could quite easily live longer and with much greater quality of living. Now when you boil that down, that is worth a lot. And that's what you have to show your potential clients what they will get, and why it's worth having you as their coach.

2. Does the client know the value of you? You need to ask the client questions that are going to help them understand what your value is, and the results you bring to them. This is getting upfront and real and stems from the last point. Knowing what the costs of the client's problems are and the value of a solution.

What is this costing you in your personal life not having this?
What will having this do for you?
Why do you want to achieve this?
How is this problem affecting other parts of your life?

3. Break free from the time-for-money trap

This is a major point of this book, and you being able to create the true end result with your business. Charging by the hour means you are selling your most precious asset – time. And that means you become a commodity by selling time. You need to charge based on the solution you provide, and why I really like this is because it means you have to deliver results.

In the health and fitness world, I see too many coaches that aren't good coaches, not willing to upskill themselves or open up their minds and eyes in how to become a better coach. I hope none of those coaches read this. I want to drive the industry up, and help coaches that deliver results, know their craft, and have the skills and knowledge to also build their businesses and success.

To do this, you need to know what it is the client really wants, what their goals and objectives are, and why the 4-step client pipeline is needed. Once you know what they need, then you can charge a rate that gives a client 10 times the value of what they get. This is how I look at my own coaching clients. How can they walk away with 10 times the better or more from this investment?

This means you need to give the cost for the whole program or service you are giving, and then have what payment options best suit you and the client.

4. Stop ranking your value on what others charge.

Many coaches reading this will be in a highly competitive environment of other coaches working in the same work-space or very close by. Then, when talking about the online coaching business, this is an international market, and you're competing with others all around the world.

Most coaches come into the situation and rank themselves on how they fair compared to their competition, and slightly up or down their rate. One of the main results I want from you using this book, is to be known for delivering a world-class experience. Which means, when paired with the last point of delivering the value and results to 10 times or more of that for what you bring to your clients, you will not be looking at your neighbour to figure out what those rates will be.

An example of this is in the online coaching world, where you can be easily swamped on social media by other coaches and fitness personalities offering coaching packages for minuscule amounts. You want to charge a fair price so that you can over deliver results and have the margin in which you profit what you are worth. My own online fitness membership is 5 times more than the common competitor than I see.

The care factor is at zero, as I never want to be competing on price, and entering a price and discounting war only ever leads to a fast-track to the bottom. I can deliver 10 times more value than my lower cost competitors with ease, by being able to have multiple specialist coaches working for me, web developer's producing custom software for my member's only site, and more. This really comes down to that I can give the client exactly what they need, in the way they need it, for them to get the results.

This also comes down the difference between price and cost. If going to a lower-priced option such as a cheaper personal trainer, though that trainer isn't equipped with the expertise or skills to get the results, the actual cost of the choice of going with that trainer is huge. You will be spinning your wheels and wasting your time spending more money with this trainer, not getting results, and give up. Or you will have to eventually choose the trainer with more expertise. Whereas if you chose the option based on results that had a higher price, your actual overall cost would be far less. You'll save money by choosing the higher valued option.

5. Offer a range of services and products.

I will admit the aim of this book is to give you a strong platform and foundation so that your coaching business will thrive, and I won't be going into this point in detail, though I wanted to serve you right and show you what's possible thereafter.

Imagine, rather than just having the one service you offer, you had a multitude of products and complimenting services that solve closely related issues. In the health and fitness world, this could be soft tissue management such as massage therapy, supplements, nutraceuticals, books, information products, group coaching, and contracted coaches using your methodology.

Not only does your income grow by more than double with ease, but you are also serving the client better to improve their situation and problem. Plus, you are building a business that is more agile and tougher to withstand circumstances that could be fatal to other coaches.

Now that you have gone through the 4-step pipeline, and armed with the additional 5-steps to further excel in the selling situation, there is the case of closing the deal, and this is simply answering any questions, concerns, or objections.

This step could simply be some missed steps that you haven't explained or shown the client, or they didn't understand as you took them through. You are not born with a gift that will have people bow down and say "yes, I want to be your client" and throw their credit card at you, so don't get duped into thinking you can do this from crappy courses that seem tempting.

Everyone is sceptical, and will have concerns before they happily come on board. You should expect this, and not take it as a kick to the shin that they do have these questions and need answers. Some people have very clear objections that just need answering to clear up any issues or concerns they might have, others just need to make sure this is the right decision, and then there are the people that will ask a hundred and one questions all very much the same, and are tire kickers, probably wanting free coaching from you and may never hire you.

The third group will be weeded out be the 4-step pipeline, and the other two types are where you can ask the right questions back and clear up the concerns. Truly understanding what their objections are and keeping note of these is powerful. You shouldn't think you're going to get to the point that everyone having a consultation or sales conversation with you is going to convert and come on board, though every experience is there to teach you and improve your business. Understanding what's someone's objections are, to why they are not buying. And being able to answer them before they even come up. That way you get to take awkwardness out of this part of the process, and you are the one that's educated to help them and take advantage of the most efficient way to convert the most prospects to clients you can, without waiting on the ones who are never going to hire you, or are not who you want to work with.

Selling without selling is naturally easy for you; you are a coach and not a salesman. Well, that's what I hear all the time, but the truth is, you being a coach means that you're able to be, and need to be an excellent salesman. It's how you're going to do what you love.

Use your own coaching skills;

You need to use your natural coaching skills to ask questions that get at the root concern, and then address it authentically. The skill you have is being able to ask powerful questions that are probing and give you the insights needed to help them. This same skill is what serves us well when prospects have concerns and objections. You are then able to get to the real concern and issue at hand, and then be able to answer the real issue directly and authentically.

Ask for their advice to solve their problem;

When someone has an issue, ask what they would need as a solution to that issue to solve it. If they think that 3 hours of training a week is too much, ask them how many they think they should be doing, and what would work for them. You can then tie together whether the solution they think they need is actually what they need, and use your expertise to educate them on what the real solution needs to be that suits them.

Give them an "if then" solution for backing up results;

Some people are hesitant to get on board with you because they want a guarantee of results. Now, we all know that this is hard to give because the results depend so much on what the client follows through with. This is where you need to put them at ease by showcasing your previous results and social proof. You can then also frame your guarantee as "if then" terms, such as, "if you follow the plan I give you, do your homework, and stick to my advice and guidance, and come to each session and give it your all, and are willing to get outside your comfort zone from time to time, then yes-you will get the results you want."

The best action for you to follow through with is using the 'objection answers' in the success sheets. This is where I will have you lay out the objections, and find the best answers to them. This is so powerful because, with just some small time investment and brain power, you are going to have the confidence and know-how for improving what's included in your marketing, and what's needed before and during each sales opportunity, instantly lifting your sales conversions.

To actually convert the client

Over years of working in commercial and private gyms, and then working with clients around the world with a wide variety of different models and businesses, I always laugh when looking back at the time when I had to 'close the deal' with clients early on as a personal trainer. I would have given them 2 of the best personal training sessions and consultations. Thoroughly asked everything needed to devise a great plan, training program, and diet, and then executed exceptional training sessions that walked them through exactly how they needed to train for fast, specific results that they wanted. And then at the very end, choked and gone down in flames when trying to close the deal and convert them as a client.

I know many other trainers and coaches suffer from this, from personally working with them to get around it, to others just telling me in the constant messages and emails I get. The answer here is that you must ask for the sale, otherwise, you will never get it, and you can use natural conversations to lead to this happening.

There are two ways that you can naturally lead into what you need at this point. Ask them "what do you want to do next?" I like asking this question because it gauges where they are at and whether they are ready to hire you or not. If they come back to you with "let's start" then you know it's all good, or if anything else comes back, you now know what else needs to be covered to move forward.

The other way to moving on to closing the deal is to create urgency with them starting and coming on board. You can begin by saying how excited you are to working with them; that you believe they are the perfect fit and want to start a coaching relationship, and hope they agree with that. Though I always want things to move along quickly, if they are not yet 'sold' on coming on board and starting with you, I want to get to that answer and move on to the next possible client. Also, if you're chasing after new clients, they can smell it, and no one wants to work with a beggar.

14 HOW TO CHOOSE WHAT TO SELL

"Be magnetic towards the right people and repulsive towards the wrong people"

This is something I continue to say to my members and coaching clients, as all too often it's too easy to get swept up in trying to please too many people, and it's not talking directly to the market you should be focussing on.

Without being crystal clear on who your target market is, and understanding everything they need to achieve what they want, and what issues, problems, and fears they are facing, you are never able to develop a product or service to best serve them, and you will never be able to effectively communicate with them so you can sell it.

Knowing your niche market goes way beyond the demographics of who you are targeting. This is where you need to get in the trenches to understand them inside and out. And the strategy and tactics that I will walk you through here and onwards has the goal of equipping you with what's needed to grow a successful business.

There is a Zig Ziglar quote that my dad wrote on a piece of paper and gave to me when I first started as a personal trainer. It was, "you will achieve what you want when you help others achieve what they want." This perfectly sums up business and how you need to look at it. You will see later in this book that when it comes to selling, it can be easy, straightforward, and natural. Being scared of asking for money or signing on a client will be a thing of the past.

This is because for someone to come on board as your client, or purchase your programs or products, you need to give them what they need. Now yes, if you are a douche-bag and sell something sneakily that isn't what you said it is, then you will be found out pretty soon, splashed all over social media and run out of business.

To go even deeper than a target or niche market, you can think of the sub-niche markets that you are able to focus on. These are the subsets and other characteristics that define the market, and often times are the gold for you being able to differentiate yourself. So, obviously as a personal trainer, 'weight loss' is a market that you can go after. It's pretty silly in my opinion to just stop there. You need to dig deeper, and this is where you can get to: over 40 male corporate executives wanting to lose weight or post-natal mothers that have had C-sections to lose weight.

Differentiation is what you need, so you have a clear marketing message, and so you can deliver that marketing message to exactly who you need.

The worst thing you can do is to try and be everything to everyone. Think how differently you would talk to an over 40 male corporate executive than to a post-natal mother, or to a 20-something dude wanting to get super low body fat. They are all completely different.

So moving from the masses to the smaller niche market will be one of the best things you can do to rapidly increase your business.

Think about this book for a second. This isn't a business book, this isn't even an online business book. This is specially written for the personal trainer or health coach wanting to grow a successful online business, which is a tiny subset compared to the other two examples.

With myself being a personal trainer for over 12 years, having worked around the world with numerous types of clients from mothers, CEOs, world class fitness and physique athletes, actors, and even to Arab Sheiks, I have been in the trenches and know exactly what you're feeling and going through. I also know exactly what's needed to build the business and success you want, because firstly I had to it myself, and then was able to teach and mentor trainers and coaches around the world to do the thing every day now.

One of the best ways for you to go about researching and learning about how to best create what people want is to ask them. With both the clients you have right now and the potential contacts you are going to make as you start and grow your online business. This is literally going to shape your business, and even for myself, I've found the ability to be agile and pivot with what I offer, the marketing messages I use, even to the brands I grow have been due to the feedback I was receiving.

This can be looked at in two ways, and this is learning from your current clients and then learning from yours leads. So let's cover both of these, as they are important, and why I've given you access to a private coaching episode in the bonuses.

Your current clients are with you for a very specific reason, especially the ones that have stuck around for a while who are going to give you insights that no one else can give. This is where myself and my members create, gather, and use feedback that can transform your business.

If you just understood;

- Why did they first come to you?
- What made them so happy to sign on with you, over all the other options?
- What are the biggest benefits of being with you?
- Why would they recommend you to others?

These four questions which are very close to what I show my clients to produce outstanding sales testimonial videos, are giving you the feedback that you can take to build your business 10 times faster.

This is the information that you can use directly in what type of content and messaging you focus more or less on. What the key areas are you need to highlight to make people attracted to you and your offer, and how to have them sign on with ease.

When looking at how you can gather critical information from leads, one example that works perfectly is using one powerful question when somebody first joins your email list. This is when someone will sign up for some piece of value you are offering, and in that first or second email, you ask them to "hit reply" and answer one question that can give you insight into why they signed up, what problems they are having, what they need help with, etc.

For my own online fitness businesses, I have thousands of responses saved and have used these to create new products, develop videos, podcasts, articles, and change branding and messaging.

The biggest problem you can have is being too 'inside your own head' and not truly tapping into what the people want. And this goes perfectly into designing your 'signature system.'

Your Signature System

This is what makes you unique, and how you deliver the world-class experience and results for each of your customers and clients. And all too often, this is where I see so many people go wrong in the online business world, as they are just imitating others.

A perfect example of someone not understanding how to design and deliver the needed experience to achieve the best results is with so many people wanting to build membership sites. Thinking that the more information they give, the more value potential customers see in it and the more sales they will make.

This is not true… As all your clients are coming to you to get results. Just like walking up a mountain, do you want a huge, oversized bag to slog up the mountain, or would you rather a super-light day pack that you can easily skip up with. This is just like what your clients need to get the results they want. By overwhelming and overloading them with 'stuff,' you've made it harder for them to get results, and will eventually set them up for failure.

If you truly know how to get results with your target market, and you understand how they need to be given what's needed for them to have the quickest and easiest results, then you are on the path to creating a product or service that will have your clients raving about.

Again, this comes to back to understanding simple and key concepts that will separate you from your competitors and have your target market choosing you as their answer. Take your time to answer these questions;

1. Who do you want to service?
2. What do you want to provide them?
3. Which of your clients rave the most voraciously?
4. What is your unique ability that separates you from your competitors?
5. What is the 'gap' in the marketplace that you can fill?

The truth is, if you haven't answered these questions with clarity, then you're going to struggle to get going. This is exactly why I'm tying in together the more advanced strategies and tactics, but never losing sight of the powerful basics that creates your foundation.

This is also why you cannot force your product on the marketplace. There is a difference between what people want and what people need. And this is also why you need to educate people by using the remarkable content we've already covered previously. When someone understands the true problem they have and what's needed to solve that problem, then as a bonus, you were the one that gave them the help with all of this, you will naturally be seen as the answer.

An example that I use in my fitness business is women who are struggling with stubborn fat. Now the main stream media has them thinking that cutting out the carbs, dropping calories, and ramping up their exercise is what will have them shedding off the unwanted pounds. The real truth is there is so much more at play here to them getting results. Their hormonal environment and interaction of hormones and nutrition, the impact of inflammation and stress on how their physiology operates all tie in together with the ability to burn body fat for fuel and being able to maximise that process, or their body storing more fat.

So by giving them easy to consume information that walks them through to understanding what the real issue is, and what the fixes are so that their bodies can lose weight and re-shape, when it comes around to presenting the offer that gives them the coaching and plans needed to make this all happen, the sale is able to happen with ease.

Truthfully, if you look at how I've put together this book, and especially with the bonus guides and training episodes, it's done not only to walk you through step-by-step but also to only give you what's needed. I could have easily doubled the size of this book and given you hundreds of hours of audio and video coaching, but that wouldn't give you fast and effective results for building your business.

15 HOW TO SELL YOUR PRODUCTS AND PROGRAMS

"If you're heading west looking for a sunrise,
I don't care how much hustle you have, you won't get there."

No matter what business model you choose and what you are going to be selling, there is a foundation of what you need for it all to work. From eBooks to the (overdone) 12-week programs, to membership sites, online personal training, and the many more options it all comes back to the fundamentals.

This is where 'newbies' can get swept away with the more advanced strategies and tactics that will not get you the traction, following, or sales process needed. If you are starting out, and earning under $100k a year with your business, the process is simple. You simply need to create a high-converting offer and use your direct and closest means in getting this message in front of the right people.

This does not mean going into advanced re-marketing tactics, webinar funnels, email behaviour segmentation, and the list goes on. Now these more 'ninja' tactics are certainly powerful and very useful, though without the foundation of work you will literally be spinning your wheels and wasting time and money for the possible outcome of never making it work.

One of the biggest reasons I decided to make the decision in dedicating the time and effort to write and publish this book, was because I am contacted on a weekly basis by people that are flat out struggling to make their business work. The common scenario being a personal trainer that wants to get out of 1on1 training in the gym, or at least have a strong online business on the side to give the security and freedom to allow themselves and possibly family the time and lifestyle they want. Giving you one resource that can outline and walk you through what you need to follow through on, plus giving you the additional resources to make it happen.

Though the problem is that they don't have ever make it happen. Always jumping from one tactic to another, one snippet of resource to another. Now, don't get me wrong the 'self-help' method to personal development is good, but when you're not truly taking action on what you need it's wasteful. This is just like someone wanting to get in amazing shape and have low body-fat. They can be focussing on nutrient timing or peri-workout nutrition, but if they are not nourishing themselves or training properly, it's all a waste of time. This is also why when I was a physique coach, whenever I had someone approach me to start training with me, I would always ask if they were using any other coaches or advice.

Whenever someone came back at me saying something along the lines of, "yeah I have another coach, but I'm not happy with the results, so I want to bring you on now as well," I always had to refuse them. It was not only out of respect to the other coach but also for the potential client, as trying to follow two different plans and points of view will lead to sub-par results.

This is now where I want to give you what's needed to take action on creating, selling your products and programs, and building your dream business.

The bottom line of you having a product to sell is that it needs to be a step-by-step guide to solving their problem. In the simplest way possible, they want to be able to have the solution, and that's exactly what you have to give them. This first rule is broken more times than I can count when clients and members first come on board, and where the following chapters are going to make sure you never have these problems.

Think of this as a 'plug-and-play' or a 'done for you' solution, because when you get to the designing and actually creating part of this book and in your business, this is how your blueprint will be. This is also why I flip on its head the order in which you go around building your online business.

If you piece together first what is actually going to sell, even going to the lengths which these days online you can. Testing what will people buy, and what will fails. As surveys are fantastic for gathering research and feedback, the best feedback of all, is if someone clicks on the buy now button and actually purchases. This is why a soft-launch and even beta-groups are two methods I use and use with my members so that when it comes to unveiling to the public and even running paid traffic to a new offer, it works, and works really well.

There is no way I could not include this next section in this chapter. I would have failed you if I left it out, as the power of words whether it's coming through written like a blog, sales page, or video. You are ultimately always selling. You are selling the fact people should be choosing to eat better foods if you shoot a video talking about nutrition, you are selling people to start training properly when you shoot a workout video.

And, you are selling people to sign-on as a client or purchase your product or program so you can give them the ultimate solution that they need. This is why when you are building your online business, that you have to maximise the power of your words, and this is called copywriting. Copywriting is the art and science of communication to have people take action. Obviously, I want to help give you this power, in the name of good. I don't want anyone taking this and using it to sell shady, false, crappy quality products or services.

You are going to have an outline of how you can create copy for your sales pages, and sales messages, which can easily flow into how you structure everything else. This even goes into how you write article blog posts, how you structure what you say on videos to podcasts, all through the different mediums.

Your copy should;

1. qualify the person that they are the right fit for what you have.
2. Create credibility for yourself, and position yourself as the person of authority to give this.
3. Showcase social proof of others who have achieved results from what you are presenting.
4. Answer the objections the reader/viewer will have when going through your message.
5. Show the benefits and the features they will experience from what you have.
6. Give an incentive to now (I will talk more about the laws of

influence and how urgency and scarcity are so important).

Even on top of this you want to guarantee their satisfaction, and wrap this up in a clear, simple, easy to consume the message.

Now for you to start piecing your sales message together.

I will argue that the headline is the most important part of your sales message as this determines whether or not the person clicks to view what you have. Especially in the online landscape, the constant bombardment of new things to click on, view, and do is endless. Especially as when we are talking about selling on platforms such as Facebook and Instagram where we can be endlessly flicking your thumb, scrolling down, it's a short second you get to attract attention and have them made the decision to click on it.

Marketing guru, Ted Nicholas, has been responsible for writing ads that have produced over 1 billion dollars in revenue. Ted says, "The headline is responsible for 80-90% of your results." So that's how important it is that you get the headline right.

One of the most important points for your headline is to prime the person for what's to come. You want to be magnetic towards the right people, and repulsive towards the wrong people. This is really important, as you don't want people clicking through to your sales video or page if they are totally the wrong fit for it. You are not going to make more sales by luring the wrong people onto your page, and especially when you turn paid traffic on for your sales messages, this is the most common scenario of people wasting their money.

As having the examples to use is one of the best learning resources when starting to write headlines, I've included in the bonus section an excellent list you can use as templates. Though rather than just copy and pasting from the templates, be sure that you are talking about the benefits directly to your prospects, and using their language.

Just like the example I've used before, you would use completely different language when you were selling diet and meal plans to a post-natal mother, than to a late twenty's male wanting to build muscle.

After the headline, you then have the sub-headline. This can be very useful to help give further explanation of the major benefits, and who it's for. Remember, people will in the majority skim through your message or sales page initially. This is why in a written sales letter or blog, you use catchy subhead lines and bullet points.

You then have the introduction that can also include injecting credibility into why the person will want to listen to you. "Why should I trust this?" is a question that will be pulsing through the person's mind that you need to answer. Also, using images of social proof where in the health and fitness world before and after's can work so well.

Even in videos the introduction to the video and who you are is a short spiel that will highlight the credibility of yourself and the information to come. You can use the 'lower third' caption which is like when you watch the news, and someone is being interviewed. Their name and title come up. I do this with both my business mentoring and online fitness business with slightly different wording to suit what I will talk about.

Then comes the social proof and testimonials part of your message. This is important, especially when presenting the offer to make the sale, and even in the messaging leading up to the offer to buy as you want to show what you have works. But especially, you want to answer the question in your prospect's head that is, "does it work for people like me?" An example of this would be a post-natal mother; she would want to see images and videos of other mothers that have gotten results. Obviously, if you're selling a weight loss product and you are drawing in post-natal mothers to your offer, yet you are showing results from younger males, or anyone that the prospect doesn't relate to being in the same situation as, then there is a disconnect as to whether they think it's for them or not.

Collecting video testimonials is powerful, as the prospect can further relate to the person giving the testimonial, and setting the scene and having the client or customer answer the right questions is the first step to making sure this works for you. Because if you ask someone "for a testimonial," you'll likely receive some nice words, but it doesn't give you the material needed to help showcase others to jump on board.

A few important questions I use and get my members to use effectively are:

- Why did you start or come onboard?
- What were the results you have gotten?
- Why would you recommend others to join?

Some bonus questions for them to answer would be:

- Were you skeptical about this at first?
- Were you surprised by the results?

These questions perfectly set up the right type of answers that a prospect needs to hear to know whether or not it's right for them.

There is no doubt that from the headline to the end of your sales page or video, your 'incredible offer' needs to shine through and be clear and simple to understand. Your aim is to craft an irresistible offer so that when the person that has the problem you and your product and service is solving, they would be nuts to pass it up.

This is where outlining the benefits and features of what you have is so important, to make sure they know it's giving them exactly what they need.

The 'features' that you will list out is what people mainly focus on; this is the logical part of the brain that consists of the 'stuff' you are giving to them. These are important, though the benefits are where you need to really shine. This is the emotional part of the brain when highlighting the benefits, as you want to easily show them what they are getting.

There is a difference between getting a meal plan, and getting a "meal plan to save you over 5 hours per week on meal prep, and have you lose 2 pounds per week." You can see in this quick example the benefits are what really make it powerful.

The next step is overcoming the objections that the prospect will be asking themselves as they go through your messages. The first part to understand with this is that they will be coming into this with scepticism. Expect it!

Everyone has been burnt, or hasn't gotten results from buying something before, and especially in the health and weight loss space where the fads and lies are thick, our guard is constantly up. This is why we use the introduction, sub headline, and credibility to help them lower it.

This is where an important step is to first list out all the 'whys' someone would not buy or take action on what you are presenting. Truly understanding your market and where their scepticism may lay is then going to help you pre-answer their questions. And remember, there are pro's and cons' to a sales page or sales video. The cons are that you can't have the direct rapport building and question asking like you can face-to-face with someone. If I was in person talking with you, I can easily find out what you're looking for, and find out why you can't buy by asking you, and then answering those objections. The positives of a sales page and video is that it is scalable, which means you can produce it once, and then 100,000's of people can be consuming it all over the world, and it takes no more effort on your behalf. And if you design the copy that you use to cover all the main areas I listed out before, you're able to showcase that what you have is for them, and answer the common objections that they will have.

The final piece is having a call to action. This is important for absolutely every single piece of content that you produce. All too often, I see people producing content but failing on this one step can put the brakes on your business growth. Even if you produce some content and all you want them to do is "comment below" or "share this if you liked it." Getting engagement is critical to help build relationships with your following, and also to further broaden your reach. As the social media platforms and search engines increase your rank with social engagement, which simply means the more shares, likes, comments, etc., that means your content will be shown to more people.

This is exactly how things go 'viral,' and millions upon millions of people will view content as it is constantly being engaged with and shared, it's pushed in front of more and more people which continue the cycle. Through the call to action, especially when it's time to make the sale means that you need to make it clear what to do. As even with the face-to-face personal training world, the biggest fear trainers and coaches have is the conversation about 'selling,' they often don't ever ask for the sale.

Creating a type of urgency around why they should take action now is very important. Even with physical products sold on the internet and e-commerce, "cart abandonment" can happen between 50-60% of the time. Which simply means, someone has selected all the products they want, and literally in the last steps of confirming and paying, they have left the site. That means that you can lose over half of your sales by not having the right call to action and urgency to act now. Though a word of warning is not to be scammy about adding fake urgency. For example, saying there is only 4x left – where really you have an infinite supply, will soon have you looking like a douche-bag. When I run fitness retreats, seminars, or courses, the need to add urgency is real. As there will only be a very limited amount of spots available, I have to make that clear in my copy, so they don't miss out. But even more, rather than everyone waiting until the last minute to buy, I can add further urgency by adding in an early bird pricing bonus. So by saying if you buy before X date and time, you will receive a discount or further bonuses, I've been able to engineer further scarcity and urgency.

I have many coaches using this for numerous types of programs and products that suit, as also adding in extra bonuses means you can solve further issues, and communicate to people what more you can do for them and further increase the benefits.

A simple ad copy formula for you is below, as I want to make sure that you can take not only this book but even this chapter alone and put it to use straight away.

Simple Sales Copy Blueprint

1. Headline
2. Subhead line
3. Introduction and credibility
4. Testimonials
5. Incredible offer
6. Bullets showcasing the benefits
7. Overcoming objections
8. Call to action
9. Guarantee

Before I leave you to finish the book and even start writing your first proper sales copy right now, I want to give you advice that I've been able to learn from some of the best copywriters and online marketers.

Firstly, you will need to practice this skill. This is something that you only get good at by doing. Yes, you can read tons and tons on copywriting, though the real magic happens when you just write. Especially as your knowledge around the target market is so important. The second piece of advice is that you need to think about your sales page or video as a slippery slide. The whole goal of the headline is to get someone to click on the link to further read it, or just to take them to the next line. The goal of the sub-headline is to get them to the first paragraph, and onwards. Just like a slippery slope, you want to start them off at the top and make it easy and enticing as possible to keep going down.

16 YOUR SIGNATURE SYSTEM

There is no way about it, you have to deliver not only great results but an exceptional, world-class experience. I make it very clear that my aim is to only work with high-end coaches that want to create massive success, and this comes about by giving each customer and client what they want and need, plus more. Yes, I do lecture and deliver courses to show personal trainers how to be more effective personal trainers, especially in the realm of physique coaching.

As a physique coach, the role is to deliver the guidance, advice, and hand-holding needed to have each client overcome their own obstacles, and equipping them with the tools and know-how so that their bodies transform while at the same time not sacrificing their health.

We talked about the power of referrals in part two, and you cannot 'engineer' referrals unless you have an outstanding product or service, and then even tie that in with an experience. And I keep referring back to it as an experience because you need to give people just that. Not just a diet, or training plan for an example as a personal trainer, but over delivering and making it easier, faster, and more enjoyable along the way to attaining those results.

Even online retail clothes stores get this (the good ones do), as your package when delivered comes in a great looking box, there is a hand written note for you inside, and then you are even followed up with an email or a phone call, later on, making sure everything has been perfect for you.

You need to engineer and create this in your business, and turn it into a system so that it's easily repeatable as your business and customer base grows. This, then, will have you going viral, turning your customers into your own walking billboards, spreading the positive word about you and having boat loads of more clients coming to you. And, arguably the best marketing and sales avenue is from a referral. If I were half interested in hiring a personal trainer and a friend or someone I respected spoke highly about a personal trainer, explained why everything was so good, and flaunted the results, I would end up on the doorstep of that trainer, credit card in hand, ready to start. Referrals are so powerful because of the social proof aspect, you want to know someone else has got the results and had everything work out fine, so it's a proven path for me to take.

The other important fact about how you need to create the results with your clients is that it needs to be scalable. Is it minimizing the time of you personally needing to be involved and at the same time maximising the results for the clients. Then there is, is it maximising your profits and business growth. Pretty simple, when it's laid out like this for you and exactly why I want to spell it out for you, so you can have the easy steps to follow to make this happen.

Let me drill it in for you, and ask yourself these questions about how you work with your clients and deliver results for them;

1. Does it minimize the time I am involved in the process?

2. Is it scalable – What's the limit of clients and capacity I can take on, or is it unlimited?
3. Does it maximise profits?
4. Do all the processes maximise my client's results?

Question two is where we first started this book together, as this is the foundation of the time-for-money trap. There are only a limited amount of hours in a day you are able to see and work with clients, and by you selling your time, means you're selling off your most important asset, that's also very limited.

Being able to have yourself step out of your business and know what will happen is a very important question. Something that rocked home for me when I attended a business conference in Bangkok. The person presenting had just sold and exited his business and was teaching on the whole process and do's and do nots with it, when it came to the question that you must also ask yourself; "can you walk away from your business and it still grow and prosper?"

For the massive majority of you reading, I know the answer will be a no, and that's ok, but it comes to the spearhead of what are you going to do about it? Are you going to be stuck in this trap anytime you want time off, get sick, have a holiday, or even want to move and live somewhere else, it's either not possible at all, or you will lose money from not being there.

What I am giving you here is going to get you out of this problem, and my focus is to have you attract and convert new clients and be able to do so under a new 'model' that gets better results for every client as it maximises your potential, growth, and profit.

So now, it is time for you to create your Signature System, and have the process that blows the socks off your clients, delivers world-class experiences, and has you known as a mini celebrity for it.

Your Signature System is the process from once a client signs on, it delivers them the results that they came to you for until they no longer need to work with you. Now, I am not going to be going in depth on the process that will have you forming lifetime relationships with clients and lengthening the lifetime customer value of a client, as this book has a specific purpose that I have walked you through.

Those concepts, along with more advanced strategies and tactics, plus more will come soon enough in another book and honestly is also what I just show my own members. This is so you are going to make a name for yourself, become that mini celebrity and cement in you being the 'go to' and number one answer so clients are flocking to you.

It astounds me, how little thought this morally gets put in by coaches as this is the actual doing part, and what they enjoy. The entire Parts 2 and 3 cover the marketing and sales section is the road bump for many, but now that you know how to bring in new clients, it's time to use your skills in a precise way so that you create the success you want, by giving your clients the success they want.

I see a lot of the time with my own coaching clients that they have been so wrapped up in getting new clients, they forget the value of the clients they already have. Every single client you have now has put their faith and hard earned money into you, and is a potential source of increased revenue, potential referrals, and even the creation of new programs and products from the work you do with them.

The average value of each client is calculated by knowing the average number of engagements over the lifetime of the client with you, multiplied by the value of your average engagement, and then also add on the referrals from that client. This will give you an amount of how much an average client will bring in for you.

Now understood, at this time, you don't know the average number of referrals a client will bring in, but this is exactly why I have walked you through the process of engineering that process, and also having a good idea of how long a client usually sticks around for you. This Average Lifetime Customer Value is a number you want to keep looking back on and improving upon.

The other reason I bring up the power of keeping the focus on your current clients and not just trying to chase down new ones, is there are 3 main ways to grow your business.

1. To have more clients
2. To increase the number of engagements with you. For example the number of training sessions per month with you.
3. To increase the engagement price. For example increasing your hourly charge or session charge.

This means two-thirds of your potential to grow your business is through the clients you already have. An important point I wanted to hammer home for you again, so you soak in and use this part of the book, as I know many would have come to this book through the lure of just getting more clients. That's absolutely going to happen, but let's be true entrepreneurs and maximise every angle.

The side effects of keeping focus on your current clients also comes through;

- Having the value of an extra testimonial
- Potential introductions that can lead to new opportunities and relationships.
- Increasing your reputation
- The value of what you learn from working with that client
- Being able to produce other products and programs from the work you do with that client.

You now see how the value of a single client easily snowballs into so much more that what you could have thought was just a weekly payment.

Pareto's principle, or also known as the 80/20 rule says that in relationship to your clients and your income, 20% of your clients will give you 80% of your customers. In the fantastic read that I highly recommend 80/20 sales and marketing, by Perry Marshall, he also highlights so well the concept that there is an 80/20 in every 80/20, which means that broken down again, 6% of your clients will deliver 64% of your income.

After reading and applying this book multiple times and with all my businesses, there is great power behind knowing and using this principle, and there are two ways you can easily use this. Firstly, this means that you need to have a range of offers, even if this was a tiered offering with greater amounts of service, value, and exclusivity with working with you and other value adds.

You could have three offerings, a 12-week training package of just 1x training session per week for $900. The next offering could a

12-week training package of 2x training sessions per week, plus their diet and training plans throughout the entire course of the program customised to them for $2400. The next offering could be a 12-week package, that includes 3x training sessions per week, customised diet and training plans, pre and post workout nutrition supplied for every session, once a week soft tissue management and massage for the cost of $4900.

I've given you the example above all around the same concept of a 12-week package, so that what's included is changed. Now, clients before have said to me, 'what if I don't offer massage (or any other service or product)?'. That's perfectly fine, hire someone else to come in and have everything work and be managed under the umbrella of your business. Technically this works out as you can hire a massage therapist for $60 an hour, but in the way you have broken down your package and rates, you're charging them out at $90 an hour, so you're making a profit from this.

The huge benefit for the client is everything is taken care of, it's easy and simple and they are getting the results they came to you for. There are the people that will just take the lower offer as it suits the economics and budget, and there are the others that want the crème de la crème offer. The other fact is that if you set your marketing up properly, with the design to focus on bringing on those 'Rolls Royce' clients, you will offer that top package in the example plus more.

You can take it further, and deliver greater value and world class experiences. I now have one fitness business that is focused on deluxe health and wellness retreats here in Bali. I have great trainers come on board to work in the business, and can offer up to $7000 packages. I have other clients that do the exact same thing and run 2 to 3 retreats a year as something different and to cater to their top end clients. Adding this on adds an extra $20,000 profit per week for them. I have another great friend that runs retreats, and she charges up to $30,000 per person, per retreat. This is to show you that you can take it up a level, and it's about giving the right solution to the right person.

You need to set up in your 'signature system' what are the offering levels you are going to have. What does the client need to get the results they come to you for, and how do you make it easier and faster for them?

DELIVER WORLD CLASS VALUE

It was a strong theme that I wanted to hit home with you before, and it's because this flows into you creating raving fans. You don't just want clients, you want raving fans that turn into a tribe that grows your business for you. Here I want to open up some questions that initially lots of coaches don't like because it exposes open wounds, but be brave enough to see them, and then we can work through them to create a strong growth business.

We talked about Average Customer Lifetime Value before, so here I want to ask you: How long does your typical client work with you? If it's a couple of weeks, even to a couple of months you could have a massive leak in your business this is pouring away money. Now, don't get me wrong, there are the types of clients that come to you for a very precise and specific result. I used to work with a lot of performance athletes, and then my strong point is physique athletes and models. So they can prepare for a certain show that might be 16-20 weeks away.

The way you have to look at this is how else can they stay apart of your business and you give them value needed. For example, being able to have an on-going support and guidance membership that means its painful if they leave because they then lose access.

Of course, that's why I know how it works and the true benefits of them staying on board. Now, the offer or package might change, they could go onto an 'off-season' rate as you don't need to be checking in as often as you would if someone was weeks out from a show.

Then you need to ask yourself: How many referrals does each client send your way? If they are raving fans, then a constant stream of new clients should be coming your way. This could just be as simple as engineering a process so it's a system to give your clients the right incentive to remember to refer you to others, to reminding them after your engagements. It could be that you're not getting the greatest results that they expect, so aren't singing your praises, which is a real problem that needs to be fixed.

And this can be done by you piecing together the perfect signature system that will have them achieving results, and you giving them a world's best experience that blows their socks off. This last point also closely relates to the next question. How many clients give you testimonials? For this is they are living what you are doing and what they get from you, then they should be easily doing so when asked, or even naturally providing you with social proof.

I see key traits that run through all successful coaches, and these can be simple tweaks and changes from your end so that your clients are getting exactly what you want. A big factor is creating the right environment for your clients so amazing results can be had. By you knowing what's needed for them to believe they are making breakthroughs, and having amazingly valuable experiences you can tailor everything around them to make this happen.

By constantly checking in, seeing if they are creating amazing results, you can make the needed changes as you move along. The key here is open communication, which boils down to simply asking questions and truly listening to the response. Caring about them enough to put your ego aside and take a stand to help the client achieve ambitious aspirations. By you having presence and focus in every interaction you have with your client. We have all seen it before, and I cringe every time, from all the numerous gyms I've trained at around the world and especially the commercial gyms where I cut my teeth for 8 years. A personal trainer clearly having no interest or respect for the client, either texting on their phone midway through their set, checking out the new girl in her tights, or just day dreaming.

I expect you wouldn't be doing this at all, though it's the perfect example of giving the time and energy for your client through all engagements you have with them.

By being open and honest with your clients, and not trying to come across as a know it all 'guru,' you're able to easily ask questions about the value your clients are getting from you, feedback that you can eat up and use to better every part of your business. This is getting advice to be better in every facet of you and your business. And especially from truly understanding from that very first interaction with your client, by getting to know how great results are defined by them, you can constantly bring it back to making sure that happens. Know what the specific goals are for them, and how they want it.

How Much Should Your Charge For Your Product

This is a stumbling block for so many, and something that can go so wrong and have you losing a lot of money. The price of your product depends on so many things including;

- The value of the product
- The perceived value of the product
- Whether or not you have back-end products of higher value that follow
- The amount of credibility you have with your prospects
- Your offer
- The effectiveness of your sales copy

And then there is one more that could be the most important. And this is your mindset and belief of what you are delivering.

The simple truth is that if you don't believe you are producing and delivering a $2000 program, you won't sell a $2000 program, and could be only selling for $200 and hence losing $1800 every time that you do make a sale. Often times, this is also why you and others can struggle to sell, as the mindset is completely off. As a bonus, I've included an episode where myself and Kat Loterzo talk about the power of your mindset and the practical aspects of how this turns into your everyday actions. Also including us talking about the difference of the mindset with entrepreneurs earning under 6 figures a year, to over 6 and multiple 6 figures a year and even taking the step to 7 figures a year.

This is an important truth to grasp, as with every client I work with I ask "how much money do you want to earn?" The response is usually a number that doesn't come with any conviction or belief behind it. So then we go through the steps of knowing how much you want that gives you the life you want, then the steps to being able to earn that amount.

Now, I will put my hand up first and admit that I learnt this lesson the hard way. And I realised I had literally lost thousands of dollars all due to my own belief and mindset, so why I write this whole book and this story showing you how I stuffed up, is so you can avoid it, and fast track your own growth.

I was in Bangkok for a business conference, the conference was held just for location-independent entrepreneurs, and the hotel that it's held in became a hive of high-level entrepreneurs all learning and growing together. Thankfully John Logar was there as well, and if you tune into the Ask The Pro podcast, you will be able to get his episodes where he unveils pure gold in business building.

Thankfully we both had some spare time in the afternoon as the event was running, and planned to meet up down in the lobby to have catch up. I always love talking with John as I've been able to catch up with him at events and masterminds around the world. At this stage, we got chatting, and he was wanting to learn more about the businesses I was running. We got into detail of one of the programs, and I was explaining everything involved and a few results I've had with past clients. He then asked how much I was charging for it, and I answered $6000.

He starts shaking his head in disappointment. I thought, "what have I done wrong?" He looks straight up and says, "you're worth more Chris… what you're giving right there is at least $8000." Now I totally respect John, but $6000 for the program I was offering at the time was not a small amount of money, but I always want to learn from others. So, I had a sales call twenty minutes after we finished chatting, and thought 'what the hell.' I'll just try to sell this for $8000, and if it doesn't happen it's only one sale, I'll lose and not the worst thing in the world.

So, I finish up the sales call sitting in my hotel room and pick up my phone next to me. I text message John, "I owe you a drink." The sale was the easiest one I had ever made to that point. It was seamless. And after kicking back and thinking about everything that just happened, it struck me. It was all because I believed in what I was delivering. I knew the program was worth well over $8000, the results my clients were getting were well over 10x that, and it was working with every client coming on board. So as soon as my mindset shifted, my results shifted.

Now, I don't want you to take this story the wrong way. Don't just go and charge more just because you can say or type a bigger number on a sales page. It has to be related to what the value of it is, but the truth is, the value and your mindset of what you believe will make a huge difference with the positive results of your business long term.

So let's look at the main points I gave you before with what's related to how much you charge;

The value of your product or service:

When you put together the deliverables and what the product and service will be, your aim should be to give 10x what the product price is in value. Now I do understand when you're not talking in "I know my client will make $100,000 from this so I can charge $10,000" and when you are talking about results in weight loss, confidence, and health you need to show what the value means to them.

The customer's perception of value:

Why does someone buy a Porsche over a Toyota? The cars both carry 5 people and get someone from point A to point B. There is, though, a huge difference in quality, but also more importantly, the difference in perception of what they are receiving and the value related to that.

This is also why I'm a big believer of not just trying to cut costs and be the lowest priced option. This can be a 'race to the bottom' which often times can have you dealing with customers that are only price sensitive and are not who you want to be working with.

Do you have back-end or follow-up products to upsell?

This is where having multiple offers and following certain offers after others can work as you are able to have initial offers as a low barrier for entry, though importantly use your other upsells to increase the lifetime customer value (LCV). Your LCV is a very important number that I won't be delving into in this book, as this is more advanced.

However, having the follow-up offers that are giving your client or customers exactly what they need, give you the ability to give more value and improve their results.

Credibility with your audience:

This is why I have been showing you how to become an expert, give great quality and the needed quantity of content to showcase your message and get it in front of the right people. You need to be building your credibility not just for people to start following you or consuming your content, but so that you can sign on clients and sell products and do so at the charge that you want.

Credibility will be achieved by you getting published in newspapers, websites, blogs, and magazines, also by being interviewed and showcasing your results and knowledge.

Your offer and sales copy:

This is one of the most important aspects of your entire business. If you do not have a high-converting offer, you are going to struggle to sell. It doesn't get more basic than that, and why I've been walking you through how to develop that from the very first chapter to showcasing it again here.

Your sales copy is the communication that you have to show to potential customers, and how you get your message across. Just like the very reason right now you are reading this is because the sales copy and messaging I used talked to you in a way in which I showed you that this would be highly valuable for you to read and use.

Now, it's time you piece together what's needed in your 'signature system,' as this takes time and refining to get it the way that turns clients into raving fans, and gives you the platform to maximise your profits and minimize your manual time needed. From working with numerous coaches in piecing together their own perfect signature systems, and creating the right business model you then start achieving what you want from your business, fast. This also leads to you growing from a single coach to a business that can run without you being there.

17 SMALL BUSINESS, BIGGER PROFITS

Before we delve into this very important chapter that I truly believe will transform your business if you take it seriously, let me ask you one question, and please answer it to yourself.

How would you approach your training business if you were able to step aside, take time off, have holidays, even go and live in other places in the world if you wanted to… and all along your business is still growing and bringing in profits to your bank account?

Just like I did, you're probably thinking, "that can't happen." And it's true, it can't happen for you. Right now, you are stuck in the mud by having a job. When I used to present courses to personal trainers when I first started branching out, I would ask the audience before we got going, "who runs their own business?" Everyone threw their hand up with pride, a real badge of honour. I then asked, "who earns money if you're not seeing your client, or if you get sick, or go on holiday?" Everyone's hands drop, with reality setting in. This isn't a business, this a job. And there is nothing wrong with having a job, but if you want to grow a strong business that gives you the money you want, and gives you the ability to live with the freedom and lifestyle you want, this next chapter you need to soak in.

Once you begin to use what's ahead, you stop trading time for money and instead focus on building a company that is worth generating income for you while you do other things. Meanwhile, all these steps and actions ahead set you apart even more as the 'go to' trainer or coach in your market, attracts more clients for you and your business, and allows you to charge a higher rate for your time.

What I am wanting you to start to create are assets, something bigger than you and that lasts longer than you, plus something that you can sell. Even if you are charging lucrative high rates, and you are charging based on value and not based on an hourly rate, being a solo coach will still have a ceiling on what you can achieve. Building a team or another way you can call it is a firm. Focussing on building a firm will solve the problems of the ceiling of success you can achieve as a solo coach, and means that you can be earning money even whilst you sleep. This is the mindset that is creating wealth.

You are able to grow your success by growing two different arms of your firm, products, and team members. You are able to turn your expertise into products that can be consumed by your future customers in e-format, such as ebooks, membership sites, online training, or with physical products.

One way to look at what products you can be producing is by looking at what level of reach do you want your products to achieve. For lower cost, entry-level items, the cost factor will allow a larger amount of people to buy in, and as your prices go up for products, they can become more specialised, valuable, and reach fewer people. For example, your entry-level product could be a $37 training guide, your mid-level range product could be a membership site that's $499 a year which includes all guides, training programs, plans, assessments, and weekly group coaching calls with yourself. The top-end offer could be a private group coaching that you deliver yourself, or have other team members coach that could be $299 a week that is highly personable and gives everything the client needs for easy, fast results. You can even take it one step further and offer an ultra-high end offer (which I recommend you do – if you don't offer it, people can't buy it) that is a Bali retreat, being a deluxe health escape that goes above and beyond to perfect mix of relaxation, and transformation for 5-nights in a luxury villa, top-end activates and coaching for $4,900. I only give this example because I run a Bali escape business that does exactly this, and have many of my business clients running their own retreats around the world. You can then with that ultra-offer alone, even if you ran it just once a year make $20-30,000 profit. What if you ran 4x per year, that's adding a handsome 6 figures to your income for a total of 20 nights.

I go through these offers with you to show you what's possible, and just one idea of how each works on the other, also, in relation to how much you want to be involved with what your business offers. This portfolio of products you can put together makes you more valuable throughout the whole process, and leverages what you know and your time to grow your business, without grinding away your time.

With the other aspect, you can grow your team which can also evolve into your product portfolio. A way to start this without stressing you out by taking on 'employees' is to bring on contract coaches or trainers to serve your client's needs as they arise. This can work well, as when your client base grows you bring on other coaches to meet the demand. From lots of personal experience with growing teams of personal trainers in both Sydney and Dubai. Now it's grown to having a team of coaches working within the online fitness business.

The key with this is to have them 'singing from your hymn sheet' so your business grows and works as one. As coaches, we all have our different ways and unique personalities interject with how we work with clients and get things done. This is perfectly fine, and I always want to feed that uniqueness for every team member I have, though especially with coaching there needs to be a 'system' in place. This will stop one coach going off and advising and doing things with their clients that are totally not what you believe in. Potentially hurting your brand and business because of it.

To see how easily this comes together in real life I want you to meet a member called Brett. Brett came to me already having his gym/ facility open and was doing well, though having members on board the biggest issue he was facing was getting himself out of so many of the tasks that were literally taking up his entire day. The first things we needed to change were the offers and business model in which the gym was operating at. So we changed it so there were just two different packages of memberships, and outlined how each one could deliver great results, the members could see it was worth a high value and he would profit more from each member. This also opened up that he needed to bring on trainers to work for him, so as I usually go about vetting trainers for a business, we started with two potential trainers and had a 1 month probation period in which they had to prove that they were the right fit, After two months, we were able to go through two rounds and end up with two great trainers that were a good fit for the gym. With the new trainers on board, Brad was able to get them to start helping in creating content and social media posts and his time was now focused on fewer tasks, but more importantly on the tasks that would help build the business.

At the same time, with this extra time and help from the new team members, he was able to put together two online products, one being lower priced at $99, and another at $499 where he could create the funnel that would appropriately sell to the right people. As the gym memberships are growing and the online fitness business is selling online products on auto-pilot, we are now in the position of opening gym number two. Though I rather go about setting up gyms in a different way to what most people do.

When you talk to gym owners, or people wanting to open gyms, there is a big stress in having to invest a large sum of cash for equipment, the facility, and the setup. So in order to do this the right way, the aim is to grow the following and potential clientele in the area in which you want to open the gym and be able to pre-sell memberships before the gym opens so that you can open the doors on day one and be making the money. So this is exactly what we are in the process of doing with Brad right now.

You being the lead expert means you can bundle your expertise, and help your team members be the best coaches they can be. But never think of them as just 'minions' doing your dirty and less important work, my view is that I always want to hire people that are better than me. I want to take on superstars and give them what they need to grow and thrive, so then the business expands bigger and faster.

FRAMEWORKS FOR BUSINESS GROWTH

This exactly brings us into the need for frameworks, and how you can create yours and have it blossom into numerous products, coaching programs, seminars, training programs, and methodologies to get results with clients. You can develop lots of steps, behaviours, attitudes, habits, challenges, requirements, and competencies that lead to getting the end result that you serve.

The power of frameworks comes into how you build your firm of coaches, and how this leads to the creation of products. Both need a framework to work and be scalable, so that you can continue focussing on growth and what you are best at. This framework is an asset in itself, as you can see most of the best-selling non-fiction books are also from coaches and consultants that have delivered this type of framework. Hint, hint, this exact book that I'm giving you is coming from the framework that I created from the failures, successes, and learning from me knowing what works and what doesn't, and what it takes for a coach to go from mediocre to success in the shortest period of time.

From knowing what the problems that your target market are facing, to creating the solutions for each one, develop a rough, draft framework that identifies the main causes of the problem and how people can work to the solution.

I've even said it before, and it's to always poke fun at the mainstream, "make money whilst you sleep." Really, the truth is, to make money 24-hours a day, no matter what you're doing. How would your life change if every time you woke up, there was an extra $500 in your account for you.

The potential that the internet gives you has its power through its reach and ease of use. And there has been no better time than now of being able to reach the exact audience you want through the use of the internet. This is one reason why I am a believer that you need to set your platform or foundation being a part of your website. Driving people to your site and then easily using this as the tool to direct them as to where they need to go.

And in the marketing sense, giving them what they need, growing relationships on scale, and being able to offer the exact right offers that people want. The power that tools such as re-marketing pixels that Google and Facebook give us, and how social media is a mammoth of potential for growing your following and client base.

I won't be going into the detail of the dominance that internet marketing gives you, that is done with my online coaching programs, as so much of the coaching has to be detailed and shown through videos and presentations for the best learning so you can really apply and use it. What you do need to know is how to get started and make the right decisions, as I know through having multiple emails come to me each week from coaches that are spinning their wheels and not finding any success using the web for attracting and converting clients.

We have touched upon a possible way that your product and business portfolio can look with the ascending offers, though I want to give you insights into why you would want to choose one over another so it suits you and your business.

Ebooks and downloadable guides, such as cheat sheets, resources guides, even shorter video training, and webinars are easy to consume and give you the muscle to reach millions of people. The caveat I will give for you is long gone are the days of creating a slapped together ebook and selling it for $27 making millions. I've seen this go right out of fashion, and so it should as people want value, and it's you that needs to deliver it.

The first answer you must come to when deciding on what you want to create and offer comes from, "what will get my target market the results they want, in the way they want it?" What do they want to consume?

Is it just an ebook to read page by page, or is it videos to see what's going on, connect deeper, and get a greater learning experience. It could be just an audio so they can consume it on the run, or is it a mix so that you can incorporate many methods.

Digital products are a fantastic method to grow your business and profits, and something that can very much be turned on auto-pilot or very close to, giving you more time

Membership sites are a great model to use as a sole solution or a part of your product portfolio. The major win for this is that it can create recurring income for you. This is something I wanted to introduce as a concept to you, as so many coaches don't use or not even think about making this happen for themselves.

What if you could have money coming to you each month, and the amount only grew, and you knew ahead of time how much it would be? Doesn't this take away one of the biggest pain-points coaches can have when selling time for money, and the unknown of clients dropping off, paying this month, making their sessions or not. On a face-to-face coaching level, this is where you can build memberships and recurring income into your coaching packages, and with the online fitness business, it's where you can offer a range of value through print, video, or audio. Offering access for the given fee you choose, the subscriber gets access to a special site not available to the general public.

When putting together a membership site, most people will think about how much 'stuff' they can cram into it. "The more, the better" thinking comes in, and this is what I'm against. It's far better to focus on what is the end result my subscribers and clients want, and what's the least amount they need to make that happen.

Think about a mountain climber about to trek up a steep mountain thousands of feet up. He doesn't want to carry as many things as possible and get weighed down, it's going to make it harder for him to get to the top, or stop him from getting there altogether. He needs only the essentials so that he gets there with ease, and it's faster.

This is the same for your subscriber, give them the easiest path to achieving results, as the biggest problem people face when coming onto a service like a membership site is being bombarded with information. Too much to take in, with it being too confusing and not being able to follow through. This is where people will fall off and leave, and this 'churn' of people leaving and needing to get more is what you want to limit.

The other great option for your online business is remote coaching or online personal training.

18 YOUR ULTIMATE BUSINESS MODEL

The phrase that gets thrown around all too often trying to draw us in is, "make money while you sleep." This often gets put in the basket of scams, and get rich quick schemes, though I want to walk you through what is not taught to so many business owners and entrepreneurs, and that's the ability to look at your business model and create multiple streams of income that all work together and help multiply your growth and profits.

You're a coach, and the power you have is your intellectual property, and combining this with technology you're able to deliver to have greater solutions that are also scalable to reach a mass amount of people.

The aim of the book until now has been to get you building a following and converting those followers into your clients, and now piecing together how you are going to give each and everyone a world class experience. And I say experience for a very good reason. This is not just about a service or a product, this is going one step further, this is giving the solution that your client desperately needs and having it in the exact way they need to solve their problem.

With Fit Body Pro, the private online coaching is a high-end personalised service that is a very hands-on, guiding, coaching process to get someone into the best shape of their life. This could just stop at delivering the client's diet, training program, and protocol, like so many do, but the secret sauce is the guidance, and having the client follow the program.

A mediocre plan that's followed is much better than a perfect plan not followed, so if we combine a perfect plan that's tailor-made, with the coaching and guidance to following it, we have the answer to getting world-class results for our clients.

These days, I only have a very small amount of physique clients, which I do as I love it, though from the business aspect I have four other coaches that are working with our online clients. When someone is signed up, the entire process is designed to give them the ease of being in the know. Once you show interest, there is a video of me walking you through what the next steps are, then, you get to book-in to talk with my head coach Gavin.

Gavin will have a 20min private talk with you, covering what you want to achieve, why, in-depth analysis, and piecing together the exact plan that will be needed. Once on board, you're given access to a private membership site that only our clients get access to. Here are video tutorials, guides, and more.

Soon comes in the mail, a manual with a bunch more goodies to give them everything they need to follow the plan, be in the know, and watch their bodies change week to week. We went over the top in every aspect, putting ourselves in the shoes of a new client, and what the best scenario would look like to create this.

When you take this way of looking at 'over delivering,' and honestly this is only over delivering compared to your competition. You blow them out of the water by going the extra step, and in my eyes, it's a necessity to put this effort in. Take this thought process through everything we are going to cover on what you can deliver to your customers and clients.

Also, before we start diving into the types of revenue streams you can create, we can outline one method of looking at how this can be done. One common theme that I use, and have numerous coaches use, is the 'ascension model.' Simply meaning that you are stepping them up at each step.

Let me give you a real life example of Lisa, and then I will break it down so you can do this as well.

To begin with, you want to turn a prospect, lead, or someone interested into a customer. To do this, a low barrier to entry is the best option, and that will usually come as something easy to consume and a lower price point.

Lisa created a 12-page eBook that also came with 3 videos that focussed on female weight loss. The aim of when I had Lisa create this was that it had to be easy for someone to get their hands on, consume the information and put it to work straight away. This first product Lisa created was just $7 and aimed as a diet that would help females lose weight and manage key hormones.

The next product Lisa created was 16-week all-inclusive transformation program that included 4 manuals, diets, printable training programs, tracking sheets, and video tutorials to have the customer easily get through and use the program. This was sold for $97 straight from her website, but importantly, it was targeted through Facebook re-marketing ads and emails to the customers who had bought the $7 program.

The next offer Lisa created was her personalised 1on1 Online Coaching. This was sold for $99 a week, and was an ongoing membership. So we are creating a recurring income here with this stream. Just having 30 clients on board with just this program would deliver $3000 a week, or $150,000 a year.

Then the top offer Lisa created was a 5-day fitness retreat that sold for $3000. An intensive 5 days where she only took on 8 clients for the 5 days and delivered everything needed for a body transformation that was tailor-made for the woman. Each retreat brings in $24,000 alone of sales, and she aims to run 3 retreats per year.

You can see that every step going through her 'sales funnel' is taking a step up. The price-point jump is clearly justified with the amount of value she is giving, and the results the customer will achieve. The difference between a $7 eBook and videos compared to a $3000 5-day retreat is astronomical.

Another option of having a fully fleshed out ascension model is a membership site where you can have just one level of membership or multiple levels of membership for varying access and value the customer gets.

I'm a big fan of the recurring model, as this turns into one place where you house everything, and can bring people into. This can take away the confusion and frustration of having multiple sales funnels running, and gives you a clear income that is coming in each week.

Dealing with 'churn' which is the amount of customers that are dropping off, is all about giving them the value to stick around. Also, making it so that if they do leave your membership, it's going to be painful. Software as a service (SaaS) companies do this brilliantly, as when you use software, your data and work becomes stuck with using this software. If you leave the software, you lose the data and have to go through the pain of setting up a new one and changing the way you work to make this happen.

This is known as being 'sticky,' and when thinking about the value you are delivering in your membership, "how can you increase your stickiness" so members don't want to leave.

James Schramko, thankfully a mentor of mine who I've had the pleasure of learning numerous lessons from, gave me a clear insight that I see work with numerous businesses, including mine. "Don't just think about adding in more stuff, give them only what they need to get the result, and make it quick and easy for them."

Having a membership isn't about adding in as many videos, guides, manuals, audio episodes or anything else you can cram into it. Your customer is there for only one reason. They want a result. And it's up to you to make it as easy as possible to get that result.

I'm not going to dive into the 'tech stuff' around how to use the ascension model, or setting up and building a membership site, to be honest, there is plenty of info you can grab hold of for free, and it's a part of my own coaching program that has coaches create this for themselves with ease in under 90 days.

With my 3 companies I run, they are all based on the membership and recurring business model. Even the nutrition company is created this way, as I want to deliver world class products along with the best advice and guidance so all my customers get results. This also delves into building a tribe with each of these 3 businesses, which are all different markets, and how you need to think about it too. Creating a community is vital, especially getting the evangelists of your following which will continue to go out and spread the word for you. In the bonuses you get, I will link to an excellent article by Kevin Kelly that is '1,000 True Fans.'

What I have covered here are multiple methods of revenue streams, from online products, programs, and memberships that involve all mediums such as written, video, and audio, to online coaching, to retreats and escapes. There is also writing a book which as self-publishing a very easy and effective means of sharing your knowledge.

This can be a lot when looking at it in a small snapshot such as what Lisa has created, though this is NOT what you need to focus on right now. The power of bringing it back to the one thing is needed for your focus.

To develop your coaching solution you need to have:

1. A clear understanding of where the client is now, and where they want to go.
2. A complete outline that gives you the ability to know what has to happen to take the client to the results they want.
3. The exact process created in such a way the client gets what's needed from the support and advice, and can include such things as assessments to know how progression is moving, the exercise or actions needed, assignments and direct coaching conversations.
4. Setting up the structure to set and then track goals, and make

the needed corrections along the way.

5. Support during and after the coaching process to ensure the results stick, even after they have stopped paying you.

PART 4
THE SOLUTION IS YOU. BECOMING A WORLD CLASS ENTREPRENEUR

19 UNDERSTAND THE ROLLER COASTER AHEAD

There is only one reason why you are happy and satisfied or irritated and angry with how much money you earn. Along with why you are having the struggles you're having to achieve the business and lifestyle success you want.

And that one reason is you.

You must take 100% responsibility for where you are, and the results you produce in your life. Starting, building, and owning your own company means you need to believe in yourself when others won't, you're not looking for a pat on the back or the instant gratification that gives you that dopamine rush on the spot, you must be willing to invest the time into yourself.

At the beginning of building your business and in the infancy stage, the fact is that you are wearing many hats, doing multiple types of jobs, and planning and preparation is an important part to keep you focused.

You feel like you're spinning a hundred plates, and you are in a mad dash to keep them all spinning an upright, and the entrepreneurial rollercoaster is the ups and downs that you are going to go through.

When one of my businesses was focussed on the end of the sales funnel finishing with a sales call, I would be up from 5am to get myself ready for the day, and with potential clients already booked into my calendar. As clients were all over the world, me living in Bali, and early mornings would work well to meet the US time zones.

One morning by 8am I had done $24,000 in sales. It was the biggest day of sales to that point, and I strutted out of my office, walked across to the garden where my daughter and wife were having breakfast to tell them the good news. There was no doubt about it, I was pretty chuffed, it was the culmination of so many pieces of the puzzle coming together, especially as the paid advertising was driving high-quality traffic and the sale funnel created was doing its job where it brought in the right people.

The final touch of the sales call, it was never a hard pressure sell, was a get to know them and their situation, and simply walk through the program I had availability for. If they were a fit, it was just getting them on board and started, and if they weren't a fit or didn't meet the criteria, then I wouldn't allow them on board.

The rest of the morning and day, up until early afternoon I was feeling good, I hadn't really thought about the money, I was already deep into a project that had an upcoming launch, and then it happened. I checked my emails which I do around 1pm each day, and there was one bad email. One negative email that for some reason struck a chord with me, and made me feel terrible, then there was another about a tech issue with a website that wasn't working.

Both of these were like a slap in the face, I had to scramble to get my web developer a message with what needed to be done, and get things back online and working. I had been running paid traffic to one web page, and it wasn't even working. I laugh now, but it was only because later that night, lying down on the couch, my wife reminded me of how good I was feeling in the morning. It hit me pretty hard that I was acting like a little girl (to put it politely) and not to be such a delicate snowflake.

I had found that I was easily getting thrown about with my emotions depending on what was happening, and this is wasteful and even useless. Firstly, it's going to have you distracted and losing energy and focus to keep moving forward. There are always going to be problems, and there is always going to need to be change, so I needed to embrace it.

The entrepreneurial roller coaster doesn't have the be the huge ups and downs, with you having the proper planning and action plan and taking control of yourself, your schedule, habits, and behaviours, you will take the huge ups and downs and bring them closer to a flat line. Of course, when you have wins you should triumph and be happy. I obviously wasn't even giving myself that. I would have a win, and it would last for about 3 minutes before my head was into the next thing. Then it's about not having those lows, it's seeing it as a chance to learn something, and to get moving forward again.

You can take everything in this book, and I'm confident this is what you need to build your coaching business, but if you don't soak up this message and what I have in this part of the book, then you are going to struggle.

You will struggle because you will stand in your own way, it's not going to be a gentle, smooth ride, far from it, so rather buckle up and get ready to enjoy it. Cop each blow on the chin and turn around and get moving again.

I see all the time coaches having a pitty-party and throwing child-like tantrums that "they are working so hard and not getting anywhere," and "struggling with money and getting clients" and all I see is a 2-year old sitting on the floor throwing their arms around in a flurry of frustration, not knowing that they could easily stand up and go get what they want.

This is where you need to now bring into your life what you want and need. Soak up these next couple of chapters, and use this lesson of embracing what's ahead, and taking responsibility so that you are equipped with the mindset that will make it happen.

20 BEYOND HUSTLE AND WORK-LIFE BALANCE

"Doing something unimportant well, does not make it important" —Tim Ferriss

"Hustle" has been lost and re-placed with an unimportant myth, that I see entrepreneurs and business owners sell themselves, to only go backwards and not achieve.

To say that you are 'busy' and 'grinding away' is a self-promotion of how well you are doing, and that subscribing to the 'hustle' mentality can easily lead to being overworked, over stressed, overweight, and causing serious health issues, plus losing the mental brain and cognitive power needed to make the right decisions and execute them.

The only thing that working 60 hours a week proves, is that you have worked 60 hours a week. It doesn't translate over into massive results or any expansion at all with your business growth. This is where working smarter, and not just harder is what you need to be focussing on.

I write this chapter after just flying overseas to speak at a business and marketing conference and had the pleasure the day before to be invited to a high-end mastermind that involved an array of entrepreneurs that are 'crushing it' in numerous industries and businesses. Literally running 8-figure businesses.

There were two huge take-aways I took away from this day of masterminding, and it was a huge slap in the face of truth to myself to realign myself and fast-track to get what I really want. The first thing was that we are all standing in our own ways, and we simply just needed to make a small adjustment in lifestyle design and belief so that we can implement what we need.

From not designing your day in how it needs to be so that you can get the work done that at the moment you "don't have enough time for," to giving yourself the OK that you can put 100% effort into a project and not be afraid of it failing.

The second was a huge confirmation that everyone needs to surround themselves with exceptional people, willing to push you, challenge you and always support you. Which I will expand on in the next chapter for you.

Coming from the world of being a physique coach, when I finally saw how it translated over from getting in shape, to running and growing your business it made sense to me. To get someone into amazing shape and low body fat condition, it's not about grinding that person into the floor with endless hours of cardio and weights sessions, and gritting your teeth through horrifying diets of low calories and carbs.

The only reason people still try to get in great shape this way is because they don't know a smarter approach. The problem when people try this approach, and this is especially seen in the physique competitor world, is that their body falls apart soon after. Their hormonal environment is unbalanced, their metabolism becomes damaged, and they are soon gaining weight at 10x the speed that they lost it –only making it harder to lose it again.

For you and your business, you can't be slaving away all day, every day and sacrifice your body and your brain to make it happen.

I am not saying you are not going to need to go through long hours at certain times of your business. I see things happen in 'seasons,' As when you are excelling in one area of your life, you are inherently leaving some other areas in your life behind, and not focussing on them as much. This is natural and perfectly fine.

The reality is for me is that I am running 3 businesses, and have 2 young daughters, a wife and my own life that I need to juggle, which means 1) everything is scheduled and 2) I don't have time to waste.

A great tool that you can implement from today is Rescue Time, where you can see day by day where you are spending time on the computer and internet and give you the honest truth. Just how many hours are you flicking through social media feeds, or getting side tracked off onto other sites that are doing you no good. Not to mention, how long emails are taking you.

When people say to me, "how do you get so much done?" it's simple. When I work, I work, when I play, I play. There is no screwing around in between. It certainly has not always been this way. One of my biggest mistakes was playing with my daughters and still having my mind and focus on solving business issues. Not being present and in the moment with what truly matters in life to me.

For you, this is about setting up a schedule of how you want your day and week to look. I understand at first this might scare you off, that you are being too structured. Though this is where I find structure gives you freedom.

Include everything in your day and week that you want. For me, I have time to go surfing, or when I'm dropping my daughter at school, or having date-night with the wife, or when I'm sitting down like right now, writing this for you.

If you're working hard but heading in the wrong direction, working harder still isn't going to bring about the results you want.

Within saying that I'm going to start this with an analogy I know you will appreciate being in the health and fitness world. Especially as myself coming from the physique coaching world, as clients come to me willing "to do anything" to achieve the physique and body shape they want, there is one factor that ties across you or anyone that wants to build the business or body of your dreams has to have.

And this is the daily focussed action to taking the needed small steps that build to mountainous achievements. I know that I can write a world class diet, training program and protocol to transform their bodies, but if they arnt willing to put the grit and hard work in. They will never achieve the results they want.

I also believe that the responsibility ends with me, being the one to ensure that they do follow through, and follow through with the intensity needed to achieve. This is also why I am an avid believer that customer satisfaction first starts with customer acquisition. You taking on the right type of clients is paramount to making sure you get them the results they want. Also why I spent the time and effort in laying out whats needed in the clarity section of this book to ensure that this is followed through by you.

The number one aim of this chapter is to concrete in that you have to take responsibility for yourself following through and taking action every single day.

And when talking on this topic there is one person I want to introduce you to, and I want you to follow. Kat Laterzo is someone I love having in my life. Having had the pleasure of knowing Kat already for years as we were constantly attending the same courses around the world surrounding the fitness and strength coaching industry, even living in different cities, we were constantly bumping into each other. Kat is a phenomenal entrepreneur that is now inspiring, motivating and showing the true path to success to her clients, and she has an exceptional work ethic to producing results.

Daily, relentless, full force action that she has built an empire on, and something I took huge inspiration from and have applied into my own daily habits and into how my businesses operate.

The truth is, its not rocket surgery you building your dream online business, I've laid out the blueprint for you to start and successfully use, plus all the bonus downloads you get from having this book in your hands is further going to excel you to to achieving faster, though if you do not soak in the true meaning of taking action that this chapter is giving you… your chances for success are handicapped.

For example Kat produces content daily on multiple platforms and mediums that extends her reach, expands her community and brings in more customers. The major piece you need to take on board right now, is that you have to be a producer and not a consumer.

What do you need to be producing on a daily basis that will showcase your expertise and put your message in front of the people you want as your clients.

There are going to be days that are harder to follow through, times when you "don't feel like it" and the excuses can start to mount. This is when you design your future, as when you follow through with whats needed to create what you want, and take action overcoming any obscure and petty excuse, your now stepping up to earning the success you want. This is what Kat shows by following through with herself.

Then you need to create this as a daily habit that you will continue for years and refine into a system that snowballs to massive results. Exactly why Ive included in the recommended readying section 'The 10x Rule' by Grant Cardone, this is the needed swift kick up the backside that we all need.

Once you combine the smart and correct actions and plan, the proper business model that you need to build and tie this all together with the daily massive action that you need to take, then I know you are going to be a successful entrepreneur that will dominate the market and outperform your competitors.

21 THE POWER OF SURROUNDING YOURSELF

"You are the average of the five people you spend the most time with."
—Jim Rohn

In the last chapter I briefly touched on that I attended a high-level mastermind and the two big take-aways that I had from it

Napolean Hill talks about in his book "Think and Grow Rich" about something called a 'mastermind alliance,' and goes on to describe a mastermind group as, "A friendly alliance with one or more persons who encourage one to follow through with both plan and purpose."

This is creating the exact environment for you that supports growth, and I have a very strong belief in that is needed for us to excel.

When I first started business mentoring, it was a very one-on-one relationship, and each client didn't know of each other. As my coaching is intensive to give exactly what's needed for fast growth and to get each client to the client number, business model, income, etc. that they came to me for, I've always been hunting down how to make the entire experience better.

I'm a part of two small and private masterminds, both with a different focus. One being solely focussed on the nutrition and supplement industry, and the other being a small group of entrepreneurs where we are all in entirely different industries and businesses. I believe that these are two of the most important assets I have in my life, and being an entrepreneur as it feeds me what I need to continually grow.

You have ideas coming to you thick and fast every day, but this doesn't mean you should chase after each one. In fact, the skill is in saying 'no' and being able to put your entire focus on only the tasks and projects that truly give you what you want.

When I completely overhauled my business mentoring business along with the coaching added the community aspect, I wanted to give each of my members and clients an extra advantage over everyone else. I formed a private mastermind with the correct platform so that they could work together, learn together, and grow faster than ever.

Just like the quote by Jim Rohn I added at the start of this chapter, think about how easy and how powerful it would be for you to be constantly surrounded by other top entrepreneurs that have you as a part of an exclusive community which has a high quality of experience and knowledge.

You are able to get advisement so you never have the feeling of being alone, or can test ideas to see if you should follow through with them or not, and ever be able to learn unique skills easily of others, and find partners to cross-promote and extend your network.

Steve Jobs did.

Michael Jordan did.

And I believe that both you and I do as well. We need a coach and mentor to be able to fast-track and have the guidance, advice, and proven know-how needed to get what we need.

This is exactly why I wasn't shocked when Aaron, a new trainer that joined the Pro Circle program was able to secure a $200,000 contract of personal training over the next year. This was one strategy that we focused on from our very first coaching call. Then just two weeks later secured another contract worth $240,000 a year. There is a podcast interview on chrisdufey.com that goes deep into this.

Now, this isn't the norm with the success of my clients, though this is exactly why having someone to guide you, ask new questions, and give the actions needed that they have successfully used before works wonders.

Imagine, in just three weeks, for now, having an extra $440,000 a year worth of personal training. Imagine what that would do for lowering your stress levels, giving you a new buzz and love for your work and the creativity it opens up for what you can now go and do.

I believe in personal training, having a coach means you get the needed map to follow, and the advice to keep you on track all the way through. Whenever I prep myself for a photoshoot for a competition, I always get the advice of a respected coach to give me the outsiders input.

Continuing down the 'self-help' route to growing your business, income, and success is an unknown path that can just lead to more frustration, confusion, and non-achieving.

I'm not saying you have to join my mentoring program, as I might not be the right person or right fit for you. This is exactly why everyone has to apply before coming on board, because I need to make sure everyone fits perfectly, and I can give exactly what's needed for this person to achieve.

If you're not the right fit or you need something different, I'll happily and easily refer you onto someone else, and do so every week.

You reading this book right now proves you're taking the right first steps, but you need to continue to take more, and why I know that you joining a mastermind and having the proven advice and guidance is the perfect next step you need to make.

22 YOUR MILLION DOLLAR BUSINESS MODEL

Now comes the point where you have to take action and piece together what it is that will bring you the money, freedom, and success that you want. Throughout the book so far, I have been outlining the strategy and way to look at what will truly get you what you want, and here is where you design your business model to make it all happen.

The fundamental flaw in selling your time for money is that there is no scale. If a new client comes to me and she is already working 40 hours a week with clients and earning $3000 a week and wants to earn $6000 a week. I cannot just double their client sessions each week. To double her profits, it comes from designing a new business model that allows her to give more value to more people.

This effectively comes down to the types of clients and customers you want to serve, the type of programs you will offer, and how you decide to build leverage. This will also evolve over time as you grow, get better, build your network, refine your marketing message and become more successful and known.

I am not to give you a one size fits all, the nature of writing a book means I can't give a perfect answer to everyone who reads this in this type of situation, only my members and clients can have that type of answer. So I am here to outline and give you the options, and walk you through how to piece it together from today.

There are three verticals in which your business can be broken into to grow from here. The direct client services you provide, the client services that others provide on your behalf and the products that give you leverage.

Your Services

This scenario is what most likely you are all focused on at the moment. When most members and clients start off with me, it's not about immediately shutting down this segment of your business it's about maximising this. There's a good chance that you still want to offer direct services for clients, you're good at it, and enjoy it, it's just you want to build the rest of the business to give you the success you want.

The straightforward answer to this segment is; how much does each client pay you, how much do you want to make and how many clients do you need to achieve this?

A great example of this is a transition period that a client of mine just went through at the point of me writing this. When he first came to me, he was doing "well." All the other trainers and coaches thought he was crushing it and the most successful, he was producing great results with all his clients, he had a full book of clients However, his earning capacity had capped out and he was poor in time and the security that if he didn't work – he didn't get paid.

His goal was to build his online business to earn $100,000 a month and to half his working hours. So the initial method I used was to leverage the three segments of the business; his direct services, services that would be provided by trainers working for him, and his online business producing programs. Everything that he created for the direct services side of the face-to-face business, we were able to re-purpose and fast-track the growth of the online business.

This meant that we were able to recruit, train, and manage multiple new trainers to then take his face-to-face training time away from him so he had a specific time to grow the products and programs in the online business, yet his income still went up. The lead generation and conversion methods for the face-to-face business were all taken care of by other trainers working for him, will eventually build into an agency that he just oversaw. The online business flourished as he was able to use the assets of the face-to-face segment of the business as needed for the online.

It's a very similar story to Aaron, an Australian trainer living and working overseas. From the very first coaching call that we had together, I was able to pin-point an opportunity that he hadn't taken advantage of. Just 2-weeks later This turned into being a $200,000 a year contract of personal training, and again 3-weeks after this another contract worth $240,000 was signed. This meant new problems, and I'm always a fan of new problems as it means you're growing.

Aaron had to bring on new trainers to service all of this new business, and again we were able to leverage everything so that he could fast track the growth of his new online business that rapidly grew his personal brand and now selling multiple online programs with a tremendous audience.

I want to share this with you to open your eyes up to what is very possible, as other trainers around the world are doing this. For your own direct client services, you have to go through the steps of marketing, lead generation, the conversion process, and creating your unique system of delivering results and then grow.

What you charge is down to what you are worth to your customer's eyes. And this means being a credible expert and understanding their top issues, developing valuable solutions to their problems, and taking action to reach out to them.

Client Services With Your Team

Team building is one of the most important steps you need to make in building a true business that will work without you having to be present in the business day-to-day. A big problem that we face is that you feel 'uneasy' about bringing in other trainers or coaches to work under you and your brand.

"What if they do it wrong?" "They could completely stuff up and lose clients and ruin my brand and business?"

These are legitimate worries, but not something that should stop you taking on new trainers and coaches to build your business, if this is a true direction you need to go down.

Now, in this book I won't talk about building a team of other players and roles in your business such as personal assistants, web, designers and tech staff, admin, legal, or such like. We will just focus on the team members that are delivering client services and replacing you entirely or partially.

I fully understand that finding quality trainers is hard. From running a face-to-face personal training business in Sydney, and now having a specialised team of coaches for the online fitness business, it's taken time and a lot of learning to get to this point.

There are some key areas which you can use from today to start bringing on the right team members.

Attitude:

One of the most important aspects of any member in your business is their attitude. Are they positive, with a good work ethic, fun to be around, creative, open with their communication, and someone you want to have around and be good for clients?

You have to take the responsibility for up-skilling and training them. I'd always rather bring in a coach that is under-skilled at the time, yet has a great attitude and willingness to make it happen (and proves this) so that I can teach them the systems and ways to be a great coach.

Work Ethic:

I don't like talking work hours with my team members, even with my personal assistant we don't talk about hours of work per week. I just want the job done. With trainers, I want to know what is their goal for how much they want to earn. Working backwards, we can quickly find out how many coaching hours that equals.

There are obviously other tasks and projects to work on that will be in the realm of marketing, lead generation, converting new clients, and client happiness. We will know how much all of this will equate to, and especially at the start of bringing a new team member in, it's about giving one job and teaching them the process of how it works.

Think of the systems and processes you are creating, and then you know how to easily refine them. This saves you from micromanaging, yet gives a great outcome and ability to change as your business grows and evolves.

The Traffic Light System:

I mentioned before that I don't focus on total hours worked per week, and the focus is completing the job at hand. This gives freedom to my team members to tackle it the way they want to, that best serves the clients and the business.

However, this isn't about loading up your new trainers with tons of work, only to feel swamped, overworked, and eventually breakdown.

This is why I use what I learnt from James Schramko, who has had extensive experience in training and managing large teams of people, and this is the traffic light system.

I keep the reporting super simple on a week-to-week basis, and one question all team members answer is simply; how they are handling their work load?

Green means they are all good and can handle more, orange means that they are working well with the load, but can't take on much more. And red means they have too much and not handling the best. This gives me a really easy way to look at the end of each week how all team members are doing, and if we need to bring in new staff.

Products That Create Leverage

This vertical revenue stream of your business can be capped under 'products.' This will vary from online programs and information products to books, seminars, memberships, retreats, certifications, supplements and physical products, and more.

Many coaches that come to me want to start and grow their online personal training or fitness business, as this has the huge ability to scale. There is a difference with online personal training products and services that you need to make clear for yourself.

You can have one-on-one personal training done via your online business, which essentially is still selling your time for money. Often times, this is going to earn you more per hour, yet still has the problem in which you can't leverage your time.

One model that is increasingly becoming more popular, and that I use as well is a membership. I have a major focus on my online fitness business, the entire system and methods set up so that I can sign on new members and have the ability to give them everything they need to transform their body and health – yet it only takes a few hours of my time each week and has the ability to have 10,000s of members.

Yes, I will need to bring in new staff such as customer care staff to handle the growth of new members, and I do have 2 other coaches helping me deliver content, yet I don't need to be in it.

Another similar method is selling information products online that could be a one-off sale, where by the membership site is an information product that is constantly evolving and recurring with payments. Many opt for the one-off sale of an information product and create multiple products to then have multiple sales.

Ultimately it comes down to what you want to create, and how you best serve your customers. And this is why I went into detail in the 'Signature System' chapter of creating the services and system needed to get the best results with everyone you work with.

Gone are the days of the $37 ebook being the only thing you do, and it just being a big word document with some images. Now your delivery needs to give more value, and often times through multiple medias such as written, video, and audio. Not only does this give a higher perceived value, but when structured properly you help give faster and greater results to your customer by giving it to them the way it's needed to.

Retreats are another avenue you can go down, these tie in your direct time, team members, and the ability to create products out of this. The 'how to' to create very profitable retreats is a complete program itself that I give to my members, and with other trainers and myself running a 'fitness escape' business, it's proven that you can add $10-30,000 profit per week of running these successfully.

Selling supplements, nutrition, and physical products ties in perfectly as your customers have multiple problems they need solving, so it makes sense that you broaden your ability to solve more issues.

This is exactly why I founded My Body Blends and have a major focus on bringing in only top-quality coaches and trainers that can become ambassadors for My Body Blends and be able to supply the products to their customers and clients and create a very profitable steam from it. The trainer wins by generating huge profits at ease on the side, and their clients win by having access to top-quality products and nutrition that they need at a much better price.

When we look at your entire business model and the streamline what you can offer, there is the ascension model that each new offering working down the pipeline becomes more expensive, and we covered this previously in the book, however, now comes the time to set it up and action on it.

Now you need to decide how you break down what you want to create and where you want to be earning revenue. Decide on how much revenue you want from direct client services, client services with your team, and products.

Then you have from the previous chapter the business model in which you need to start building from today, and each of the steps that go from crafting your unique message to attract the right type of customers and clients to delivering world class value.

23 YOUR ACTION PLAN

Now it comes time where you have to apply everything that I have walked you through. The most important thing to focus on from here is taking the right action, as all too often when I am on boarding a new client or member into a program, and learning about what's broken, missing, or hasn't worked before, it's the jumping from ship to ship when it comes to actions.

I'll put my hand up first and say 'guilty' as I used to do this all the time, as being busy surely meant that I was taking strong strides forward. And this is just not the case. There is a huge difference in being busy and being productive.

There are effectively three situations you can be in right now, and knowing this from the beginning I structured what I gave you to suit all three.

You are starting out and need to pick up your first clients. You are already up and running, but need to build up to a full-book of clients, or you already have a full-book and need to leverage by creating products, programs, and a team.

If you're starting out, then the below action flow is a perfect start, even if you are already up and running, I recommend you go over these points, as whenever I do this with my clients it breaks open into a new world of where your business can be positioned and grow with ease.

1. Choose your perfect type of client and target market
2. Understand deeply the needs of your target market
3. Develop one main coaching framework and program to give the best results that is a minimal viable product – you will always improve and perfect upon this later
4. Develop your marketing message (unique selling proposition) that talks to, and attracts your target market and tells them why they should choose you.
5. Test your marketing message.
6. Outline your pricing strategy, so that you can use it moving forwards.
7. Get introductions to potential clients from people you know
8. Build your content and platform through your website and targeted social media so that you can grow your following
9. Outline how you will turn your following into your customers and clients.

Once these initial steps are taken and you are signing on new clients, there are important actions to take such as developing your strategy on how to increase the lifetime customer value of everyone you work with, how you will have front-end and back-end options for your customers, how to perfect your programs for optimal results, building leverage, referral strategies, and more (much I've already covered in detail).

There are the must-use resources that are a part you getting your eyes and hands onto this right now over at chrisdufey.com/100clientsbonus. This is where you are going to get access to the templates, guides, insights, and exclusive coaching videos that build upon everything I couldn't fit, include or best use in this book, and so you can excel further and faster by using this.

THE 'SECRET SAUCE.'

From working with and chatting to so many coaches and entrepreneurs that range from first starting out to running 8-figure a year businesses, there is a constant thread that I see that differentiates the winners and the losers. The ones that create the success they want and the others that keep 'grinding away,' yet never make the impact.

It's you and only you that stands in your way to making it happen.

I say this to every coaching client and member, "I can give you the exact map to follow, you just have to follow it."

Just like a weight loss client and their personal trainer. The trainer can give the exact workouts, diet, schedule, protocols, the lot. But if the client still goes home, doesn't do the workouts, doesn't follow the diet plan – they will never get the results.

This is why after having the experience of transforming so many lives and businesses, I write this now for you because I have to get it out. I have to get all these strategies, methods, and insights out into the world, and you being here right now at the end means a lot to me. It would mean a lot more however, if you actually follow through with it.

It's your turn now to put this into action. Exactly why I have added the bonus area that you can sign into for free by getting your hands on this book. Go to **http://www.chrisdufey.com/100clientsbonus**

And join the Fitness Business Success Circle with the private link inside once you sign up.

I'm looking forward to you joining and being able to have you create the positive impact while doing what you love.

16355494R00111

Printed in Great Britain
by Amazon